Sir John Kelyng

A report of divers cases in pleas of the crown

Adjudged and determined in the reign of the late King Charles II.

Sir John Kelyng

A report of divers cases in pleas of the crown
Adjudged and determined in the reign of the late King Charles II.

ISBN/EAN: 9783337273392

Printed in Europe, USA, Canada, Australia, Japan

Cover: Foto ©ninafisch / pixelio.de

More available books at **www.hansebooks.com**

A REPORT
OF DIVERS
CASES
IN
PLEAS OF THE CROWN,

ADJUDGED AND DETERMINED

IN THE REIGN OF THE LATE

KING CHARLES II.

WITH DIRECTIONS FOR

JUSTICES OF THE PEACE AND OTHERS.

COLLECTED

By Sir JOHN KELYNG, Knt.

LATE LORD CHIEF JUSTICE OF HIS MAJESTY'S COURT OF KING'S BENCH.

From the Original Manuscript under his own Hand.

TO WHICH IS ADDED,

The REPORT of three Modern CASES,

ARMSTRONG and LISLE —— The KING and PLUMMER —— The QUEEN and MAWGRIDGE.

As originally published

By LORD CHIEF JUSTICE HOLT.

WITH ADDITIONAL NOTES AND REFERENCES,

By G. J. BROWNE, BARRISTER at LAW.

DUBLIN:

PRINTED BY P. BYRNE, No. 108, GRAFTON-STREET.

M,DCC,LXXXIX.

ADVERTISEMENT.

MY Bookseller some Time ago informed me of an Intention he had formed of publishing the Reports of Sir *John Kelyng*, which had for some Time past become scarce in this Kingdom, and requested my Revision of a New Edition of it.—Those who have experienced his Civility and Attention, know that it is not easy to refuse him a Request, which does not materially interfere with their Pleasure or their Interests.—*Kelyng* had very early, with me, been a favourite Law Writer; and in my first legal pursuits, I read it with all the Attention of which I was capable, and with all the Industry which I possessed.—If I had no Wishes for my Bookseller, it would not, therefore, have been very hard to induce me to undertake that Office.—I consented to become the Editor. In that Duty, which has been done to the best of my Skill, I procured the two Editions which had been already publifhed, and found them to be as they are defcribed by Worral, in fact the fame. The Edition of 1739, differing from that of 1708, only by having a new Title. I very foon difcovered this, and it faved me the ufelefs Labour of Collation: But I compared all the References with the Original Authorities, and have added fome new References, not fo much indeed to Modern Reports, as to the approved Syftematic Writers of Crown Law, whofe Works had not appeared when this Report was firft publifhed.

Of the Report itfelf, it may be fufficient to fay that it was publifhed by Lord Chief Juftice *Holt*, fhortly after the Revolution, when the Crown Law became better underftood, and had affumed that conftitutional and fyftematic Arrangement which at prefent harmonizes and adorns it; and was divefted of that anomalous and arbitrary Difcretion, which before that Period had difgraced it.—*Kelyng*'s Report may, therefore, be confidered as one of the beft Manuals of Crown Law.

In confidering my Author, I here and there hazarded a Note; but the Notes have rather been borrowed from the Works of others, than from any Obfervation of my own.—In my referring

ADVERTISEMENT.

ring to the different Authorities of *Hawkins*, *Hale*, and *Foster*, I have ufed the laft Editions, I mean the fixth Edition of *Hawkins*, by *Leach;* *Wilfon*'s Edition of *Hale*, and the fecond Edition of *Foster* by *Dodfon :* I choofe to mention the particular Editions to which I refer, as in the paging of *Hawkins* there is a confiderable Variation from any of the older Publications of that Work; and as there are many Inaccuracies corrected in the latter Editions of *Hale* and *Hawkins*.

" The dull Tafk of an Editor" has been often enough obferved upon. However, as a profeffional Man, I have experienced too much of the Utility of that kind of Labour in others, not to feel Gratitude.—If mine fhall eafe the Tafk of the Student, or more fpeedily direct the Refearch of the learned, I fhall think a Vacation not thrown away, and be content with the humble Praife of Diligence, nor covet that of more fplendid or faftidious Ornament.

Chancery-lane, Dublin,
 June 1ft, 1789.

WE do allow and approve of the Printing and Publishing the Reports and Cases in Pleas of the Crown, collected by the late Lord Chief Justice *Kelyng*, and three other Modern Cases added thereunto.

J. HOLT,
JOHN POWELL,
LITTLETON POWIS,
H. GOULD.

READER,

THERE can be nothing more said to, recommend these Cases to your Perusal, than to assure you they are the Collection of Sir *John Kelyng*, Knt. sometime Chief Justice of the Court of King's Bench; the Manuscript whereof under his own Hand was in the Custody of his Grandson and Heir; Copies whereof were dispersed in several Hands, which might hereafter be published to the Injury of the Author, and Disadvantage of the Publick.—There are two *Quæres* inserted in the Margin by the Publisher, the one is in Page 13, the other in Page 41, which may be fit to be considered by the Learned.

The three Modern Cases are conceived to be of some Use, therefore are thought fit to be published; and if they shall be found to be of any Benefit, its what is desired by the Publisher thereof.

FARWEL.[*]

[*] This Preface was written by Lord Chief Justice *Holt*.

ORDERS

AN INDEX

TO THE

CASES REPORTED.

A.

	Page
Appletree's Cafe	70
Armſtrong v. Lifle	93
Aſton *alias* Raven Mary's	24
Axtel's	23

B.

Backſtead John's Cafe	13
Baſely's	70
Bedel's	73
Bever's	52
Brewſter's	23
Brooke's	ib.
Burgeſs's	27

C.

Caffy's Cafe	62
Chadwick's	43
Clarke's	33
Coke of Grey's Inn's	12, 23
Corbet Miles's	13
Copeland's	45

	Page
Cotter's	62
Cotton's	72

D.

Davis's Cafe	32
Dover's	23

E.

F.

Fabian's Cafe	39
Farr's	43
Fleetwood George's	11
Ford's	51

G.

Gardner's Cafe	47
Gaye's	35
Girling's	58
Grey's	64
Green's	74

Hacker's

INDEX.

H.
	Page
Hacker's Cafe	12
Harrison's	9
Hewlet's	10
Hood's	50
Huget's	59
Hull's	40

I. J.
Jene Jones's Cafe	37
Jones's	52
Johnson's	58
Joyner's	29

K.

L.
Layer's Cafe in *not*.	10
Latimer's	73
Legg's	27
Lemott's	42
Lisle's	89
Locoft's	30
Lymerick's	73
Lysle Armstrong *v.*	93

M.
Marten Henry's Cafe	11
Marriot's	38
Mawgridge's	119
Messenger's	70
Middleton's	27
Morley Lord's	53

N.

O.
Okey John's Cafe	13
Oliver's	33

P.
	Page
Philips George's Cafe	17
Plummer's	109
Powel's	58

Q.

R.
Rampton's Cafe	41
Raven Mary's	24, 81
Rew's	26
Roberts John's	25

S.
Simson's Cafe	31
Stanley Sir Charles's	87
Stubbs Francis's	17

T.
Thong Thomas's Cafe	17, 20
Thorely's	27
Tomson's	66
Trollop's	39
Turner's	30
Twyn's	22

V. U.
Vane Sir Henry's Cafe	14, 20
Villar's	30

M.
Waller Sir Hardus's Cafe	11
Wharton's	37

TO THE RIGHT HONOURABLE

JOHN LORD BARON EARLSFORT,

CHIEF JUSTICE OF IRELAND.

My Lord,

THE Reports of Sir JOHN KELYNG, at this Day require no Voucher. The Learning and acknowledged Ability of their original Editor, Sir JOHN HOLT, have fufficiently introduced them to the Profeffion. The fame cannot be faid of thefe Reports in the hands of their prefent Editor, who is obliged to have recourfe to adventitious Recommendation— For that Purpofe give me leave to intreat the Protection of your Lordfhip, to whofe Court the Work has a particular Relation, and whofe Attention, to even the humbleft

Cultivators

Cultivators of the Law, has been evinced in the Condescension and Favour which I have so amply Experienced, and at the same time to assure your Lordship that I am, with the most thorough Sense of Gratitude,

   My Lord,

    Your Lordship's

     obliged, obedient

    and very humble Servant,

Chancery-Lane,
June 6, 1789.

   GEORGE JOSEPH BROWNE.

DIRECTIONS

FOR

JUSTICES of the PEACE.

ORDERS *and* DIRECTIONS *to be observed by the* Justices of the Peace, *and others, at the Sessions in the* Old Baily, *for* London *and* Middlesex, *made* 16 Car. 2. *by Sir* Robert Hyde, *Chief Justice of the King's Bench ; Sir* Orlando Bridgeman, *Chief Justice of the Common Pleas ; Sir* Thomas Twisden, *one of the Judges of the King's Bench ; Sir* Thomas Tyril, *one of the Judges of the Common Pleas, and Sir* John Kelyng, *one other of the Judges of the King's Bench, and signed by them all, and Read in open Court, and ordered to be filed by the Clerk, that all Justices might take Copies by them if they please : For that they shall not for the Future pretend Ignorance of their Duty.*

1. THAT all Recognizances and Bailments taken by any Justice of the Peace, be certified into the Court the first Day of every Sessions before Noon, for that they being kept longer out, it often happens that

2 Hawk. 56.

Felons and other Offenders escape the Prosecutors, Witnesses, and Parties being wearied out with Delays and Attendance, beside many other great Mischiefs; and that the Justices of Peace who are faulty herein be fined by the Justices of Goal Delivery, according to the *Stat.* of 1 & 2 *Ph. & Ma. cap.* 13. and 2 & 3 *Ph. & Ma. cap.* 10.

2. If the Offenders appear not upon their Recognizances the first Day, the Default to be Recorded, and the Recognizance to be forfeited; Nevertheless Processes or Warrants, as the Case shall require, to go out against them and their Bail; so likewise as to those who are bound to give in Evidence, that if possible the Business be not deferred to another Sessions, in which time commonly the Prosecutors and Witnesses are taken off, and the Matters compounded.

3. That all Justices of the Peace do take Examinations both of the Felons without Oath, and the Informers and Witnesses against them upon Oath in Writing before they commit the Offenders to the Goal, and certify the same the first Day of the Sessions, that they may be ready upon the Tryal of the Felons, or else to be fined according to the Statutes of *Ph. & Mary* before mentioned.

4. That all Prisoners for Treason and Felony be according to Law, sent to the common Goal, which is *Newgate*, and not to the *New-Prison*. It being found by Experience that they are often set at Liberty there without Tryal.

Directions for Justices of the Peace.

5. That no Prisoner for Felony be discharged during the Interval of Sessions, unless it be upon good Bail taken, the Warrant or Mittimus to the Goaler to keep them until they are delivered according to Law, nor any Bail or Recognizance for Appearance to be given up or withdrawn by the Justice of Peace after the Same is taken, but be returned and certified to the Sessions or Goal Delivery, the Offender whether Justice of Peace or Goaler to be severely proceeded against.

6. If any Justice of the Peace shall take Bail where he ought not, or wittingly or willingly take insufficient Bail, and the Party appear not, the said Justice not only to be proceeded against according to Law, but likewise to be complained of to the Lord Chancellor, that he may be turned out of his Commission.

7. That no Copies of any Indictment for Felony be given without special Order upon Motion made in open Court, at the general Goal Delivery upon Motion, for the late frequency of Actions against Prosecutors (which cannot be without Copies of the Indictments) deterreth People from Prosecuting for the King upon Just Occasions.

8. That the Goalers make more perfect Kalendars than of late they have done, according to the *Stat. H.* 7 *cap.* 3. and insert not only Persons in their Custody, but also such as have been in their Custody since the last Sessions, and Bailed or Delivered out, and by whom.

Directions for Justices of the Peace.

9. That if any *Habeas Corpus* come to receive a Prisoner from another Goal, the Goaler to take notice of the Offence for which he stood Committed at the other Goal, and to inform the Court, that if he shall happen to be acquitted, or have his Clergy, he may yet be remanded to the former Goal, if there be Cause.

10. If any *Habeas Corpus* come to the Goalers to remove a Prisoner, that with the Prisoner they also certifie the Cause for which he stood there committed. It being found by Experience, that by Colour of *Habeas Corpus* to receive and remove Prisoners, many notorious Offenders do Escape.

11. That no Prisoner convicted for any Felony, for which he cannot have his Clergy (unless it be Women, in such Cases, where if had they been Men, they might have had Clergy) be reprieved, but in open Sessions, and not otherwise, without the King's express Warrant, and not by order of any the Justices of Goal Delivery, or *Oyer* and *Terminer* *.

12. That such Prisoners as are reprieved, with intent to be transported, be not sent away as perpetual Slaves, but upon Indentures betwixt them and particular Masters, to serve in our *English* Plantations for seven Years, and the three last Years thereof, to have Wages, that they may have a stock when their Time is expired; and that an Account be given thereof, and by whom they are sent, and of their Arrivals †.

13. For

---

* As to the Nature of the Benefit of Clergy, or rather of the Statute at this Day, see 2 Hawk. Cap. 23. *per totum*, & 4 Black. Com. 338.

† For the modern rule, as to transportation, see 1 Hawk. p. 244. App. 13th, per tot. and 2 Hawk. Tit. Transportation, p. 514.

Directions for Justices of the Peace.

13. For that it hath frequently happened of late, that some have been killed upon Duels, others upon suddain Quarrels in the Streets. And the Inhabitants neglect to apprehend the Murderers, or to make Huy and Cry after them, and so the Persons not only escape, but no direct Knowledge can be given who they are. And by the Law, if any Man be slain in the Day, and the Fellon not taken, the Township ought to be amerced; that therefore when any such case appeareth at *Newgate*, as it too often doth, upon the acquittal of Persons apprehended upon Suspicion, that both the Coroner, as also the Secondaries at *Newgate* be required to attend the Judges of the King's Bench, that Information may be put in that Court against the Townships for the escape, and followed *pro Rege*; and at the next Sessions at *Newgate*, give an Account what is done.

Ro. Hyde,
Orl. Bridgeman,
Tho. Twisden,
Tho. Tyrell,
John Kelyng.

High-Treason.

AFTER the happy Restauration of King *Charles* the Second to his Right of the Crown of *England*, which was in *May*, 1660, several Persons who were apprehended for the Murder of his Father, were now to be indicted for that horrid Treason, and in order thereto, the then Judges, who, at that Time were only the Lord *Bridgeman*, then Chief Baron of the Exchequer; Justice *Foster*, and Justice *Hide*, then Judges of the Common Pleas, and Justice *Mallet*, then Judge of the King's Bench, met several times, at *Serjeants-Inn* in *Fleet-street*, with Sir *Jeffry Palmer*, the King's Attorny, and Sir *Heneage Finch*, the King's Solicitur, Sir *Edward Turner*, Attorny to the Duke of *York*; Mr. *Wadham Windham*, of *Lincoln's Inn*, and myself, being by special Order to attend that service as Counsel for the King, there being then no King's Serjeant, but Serjeant *Glanvill*, Serjeant to the late King, who was then Old, and Infirm: And in order to the proceeding in that great Affair, I was appointed to make as many Queries as I thought fit to be advised upon; which, I did accordingly, and upon them, these Things following were resolved.

Resolutions of all the Judges upon the Case of the King's Murderers.

1. That it was better to try those Traitors at the Sessions at *Newgate*, by Commission of Goal Delivery, then only by special Commission of *Oyer* and *Terminer*; because then they might be proceeded against more speedily, and arraigned and tryed immediately, by the Commission of Goal Delivery, and Tales might be immediately returned at the Goal Delivery. And accordingly writs were ordered to be made and sent to the Lieutenant of the *Tower*, in whose Custody the Prisoners then were to deliver

2 Hawk. 572. Tryal at Goal Delivery, with a Commission of *Oyer* and *Terminer* joyned with it, better than a Tryal by a special Commission of *Oyer* and *Terminer*.

ver them to the Sheriffs of *London*, and Writs to the Sheriffs of *London* to receive them, that they might be in *Newgate*, which was done accordingly. And becaufe, by an Act of Parliament or Convention which fat at the King's coming in Englifh Proceedings were continued until *Michaelmas* now clofe at hand, but not yet come; Therefore thofe writs to the Lieutenant of the *Tower* and Sheriff of *London*, were ordered to be in *Englifh* *.

2. It was agreed that all the Prifoners fhould be arraigned the firft Day before any of them were brought to Tryal, and the next Day to proceed to Tryal with one or more of them together, as fhould be thought fit upon the place.

King's Council may privately give Evidence to the Grand Jury.

3. It was refolved that any of the King's Council might privately manage the Evidence to the Grand Inqueft, in order to the finding of the Bill of Indictment, and agreed that it fhould be done privately; it being ufual in all Cafes, that the Profecutors upon Indictments are admitted to manage the Evidence for finding the Bill; and the King's Council are the only Profecutors in the King's Cafe, for he cannot profecute in Perfon.

Compaffing the King's Death in the Treafon.
1 Hawk. 51.
1 H. P. C. 127.
Foft. 194.
Prin P. L. 123.
3. Inft. 12.

4. It was refolved that the Indictments fhould be for compaffing the Death of the late King (the very compaffing and imagining the King's Death, being the Treafon within the *Stat.* 25 *Ed.* 3.) and then that we might lay as many Overt Acts as we would, to prove the compaffing of his Death: But it was agreed, the actual Murder of the King fhould be precifely laid in the Indictment, with the fpecial Circumftances as it was done, and fhould be made ufe of as one of the Overt Acts, to prove the compaffing of his death.

Overt Act not laid in Indictment may be given in Evidence. This is altered by the Statute of 7 W. 3. c. 3. p. 11.

5. It was refolved that if any one Overt Act tending to the compaffing the King's Death, be laid in the Indictment. That then any other Act which tends to the compaffing

* All Law Proceedings are now in Englifh by 4. Geo. 2. Cap. 26. 6 Geo. 2. Cap 14, in *England*; and by 11 Geo. 2. Cap. 6, in *Ireland*. See fome Obfervations on this Alteration, in 3 Black. Com. 322.

the King's Death, may be given in Evidence together with that which is laid in the Indictment.

6. It was resolved that there need not be two Witnesses to prove every Overt Act, tending to the compassing of the King's Death. But one Witness to prove one Overt Act tending to the compassing the King's Death, and another Witness to prove another Act tending to the same end, are sufficient; for compassing the King's Death is Treason. And then if two several Witnesses prove two several Acts tending to the compassing the King's Death, the Treason is proved by two Witnesses as the Law in Case of Treason requireth. *Fost. 237. 3 St. Tr. 204. Sir J. Raym. S. C. 2 Hawk. 366, 603. 2 H.P.C. 286.*

7. It was resolved that if several Persons be indicted together in one Indictment for one Crime, in case some of them be found guilty by one Jury, and afterwards some of the same Jury be returned for Tryal of others in the same Indictment; it is no Challenge for those Prisoners to say, that those Jurors have already given their Verdict, and found others guilty who are indicted in the same Indictment for the same Offence; for though they are all indicted in the same Indictment for the same Offence, yet in the Law it is a several Indictment against every one of them, and the Crime is several, and one may be guilty and not another, and the Jury are to give their Verdict upon particular Evidence against every several Person, and therefore the finding one guilty, is no Argument or Presumption that those Jurors will find another guilty. *Finding others guilty in the same Indictment, no cause of Challenge. 2 Hawk. 589. 4 St. Tr. 141, 175, 704.*

8. It was resolved that if several Prisoners be put upon one Jury, and they challenge peremptorily, and sever in their Challenges, that then he who is challenged by one, is to be drawn against all, because the Pannel being joint, one Juror cannot be drawn against one and serve for another. But in such case it was agreed the Pannel might be severed, and that the same Jury may be returned betwixt the King and every one of the Prisoners, and then they are to be tryed severally, and there the Challenge of one Prisoner is no Challenge to disable the Juror so challenged against another Prisoner. And the case of Dr. *Ellis*'s Servant, *Plo. Com.* 100, 101, was agreed to be good Law, as to the severing of the Pannels in that case; and accordingly after- *Severing of the Pannel. 2 Hawk. 573.*

High-Treason.

2 Stat. Tr. 304, 9.

wards upon the tryal of *Harrison* and others, who challenged peremptorily, and severed in their challenges, particular Jurors, the Panels were severed.

(10)
Irons to be taken from Prisoners at their Tryal.
Bracton 137.
3 Inst. 34, 35.
Sum. 212.
2 Hale 219.
2 Hawk. 436, 7.
2 St. Tr. 381.
2 Hawk. 330.

9. It was resolved that when Prisoners come to the Bar to be tryed, their Irons ought to be taken off, so that they be not in any Torture while they make their defence, be their Crime never so great. And accordingly upon the Arraignment and Tryal of *Hewlet* and others, who were brought in Irons, the Court commanded their Irons to be taken off *.

Quidam ignotus.

10. It being agreed that the Murder of the King should be specially found, with the Circumstances in the Indictment. And it being not known who did that villainous Act; it was resolved, that it should be laid that *Quidam ignotus*, with a Visor on his Face did the Act; and that was well enough, and the other Persons be laid to be present, aiding and assisting thereunto.

No Year laid for one Act.

11. The compassing the King's Death, being agreed to be laid in the Indictment, to be 29 *Jan.* 24 *Car. Primi*, and the Murder on the 30*th* of the same *Jan.* It was questioned in which King's Reign the 30*th Jan.* should be laid to be, whether, in the Reign of King *Charles* the first, or King *Charles* the second, and the Question grew, because there is no Fraction of a Day, and all the Acts which tended to the King's Murder, until his Head was actually severed from his Body, were in the time of his own Reign, and after his Death in the Reign of King *Charles* the second. And though it was agreed by all, except Justice *Mallett*, that one and the same Day might in several respects, and as to several Acts, be said to be intirely in two Kings Reigns, so that in some respects the whole Day may be ascribed to one, and in other respects, the whole Day ascribed to the other, according to the Truth in the Matters of fact which were acted, either in the Life, or after the Death of the first King, yet because Justice *Mallett* was earnest that the whole Day was to be ascribed to King *Charles* the second, therefore it was agreed, that in that place, no Year of any King

---

* In *Layer's* Case, A. D. 1722. a Distinction was taken between the Time of Arraignment and the Time of Trial; and accordingly *Layer* stood at the Bar in Chains during the Time of his Arraignment. 4 Black. Com. 322. 6. St. Tr. 230.

High-Treason.

King should be named, but that the compassing of the King's Death should be laid on the *29th Jan. 24 Car.* and the other Acts tending to his Murder, and the Murder itself laid to be *Tricesimo Mensis ejusdem Januarii*, without naming any Year of any King, which was agreed to be certain enough.

(11)
2 Hawk. 333.
Bur. 1901.
S. P.

12. It being agreed that the Indictment should be for compassing the King's Death, and one of the Overt Acts to be the actual Murder of the King: It was resolved the Indictment should conclude *contra pacem nuper Domini Regis Coron' & dignitat' suas, Nec non contra pacem Domini Regis nunc Coron' & dignitat' suas.*

Contra pacem of two Kings.

13. The Question was put, whether the Recorder of London should give the Charge to the grand Inquest at *Hick's-Hall*, where the Indictment was to be found, the Fact being in *Middlesex;* And also whether Judgment at the Sessions-house, where the Prisoners were to be tryed, should be there given by the Recorder, or whether the Charge and the Judgment should be given by the Chief Judge: And it was agreed that both should be given by the Chief Judge. And accordingly this was done by my Lord *Bridgeman*, and he gave the Charge only relating to enquire of the Murderers of the late King, without mixing any other matter then to be enquired of: And after the Charge, one Indictment was preferred against all the King's Murderers, who were in Prison, and also against several others who were not then apprehended, but agreed they should be attainted by an Outlawry upon the same Indictment. And the same Day the Indictment was found, and the next Day delivered at the Goal delivery, in the Sessions-house in the *Old Bailey*, which Day all the Prisoners were arraigned, and pleaded not guilty, but afterward some of them withdrew their Plea, and confessed the Indictment, *viz.*

Chief Judge giveth Judgment in Treason.

The Day was *Tuesday*, 9th of *Octo.* 12 *Car.* 2d.

14. Sir *Hardres Waller*, and *Geo. Fleetwood*, which was accordingly recorded by the Court, and agreed by all the Judges, that it might be done, altho' the Clerk had recorded their Plea of not guilty; for the Entry is, that such a one *postea*, or *relicta verificatione cognovit Indictamentum*.

Confession after not guilty pleaded.
2 Hawk. 469.
2 St. Tr. 303.

15. *Memo-*

High-Treason.

Variance in Letters of Sirname.
2 St. Tr. 238.
2 Hawk. 328.

15. *Memorandum*, That upon the Arraignment of *Henry Martyn*, his Name being so written in the Indictment, he said his Name was *Marten*, and not *Martyn*; but the Court agreed that he being known by that Name of *Martyn*, that was well enough in an Indictment, tho' it be not spelled directly as he spelleth it.

Memorandum, That the Indictment was in *Latin*, it being preferred after *Michaelmas*, until which time, all *English* Proceedings were allowed by that Convention which was sitting when the King was restored.

And after, all the Prisoners who pleaded not guilty, were convicted upon full Evidence, and had Judgment of High-Treason.

Commissioners for Tryal, give evidence as Witnesses. Hacker's Case.
2 St. Tr. 378.
2 Hawk. 608.

Memorandum, That Secretary *Morris* and Mr. *Annesley*, President of the Council, were both in Commission for the Tryal of the Prisoners, and sate upon the Bench, but there being occasion to make use of their Testimony against *Hacker*, one of the Prisoners, they both came off from the Bench, and were sworn, and gave Evidence, and did not go up to the Bench again during that Man's Tryal; and agreed by the Court they were good Witnesses, tho' in Commission, and might be made use of.

2 St. Tr. 337.

16. Upon the Tryal of *Coke* of *Greys-Inn*, who was of Council against the King, and delivered in the Charge against the King in the Traiterous Court called the High Court of Justice; he objected that he did not draw up the Charge; but he only acted as a Counsellor, and did only speak Words to have the Charge read, and demanded Judgment against the King; and he said Words did not make Treason.

Acting a Counsel, not excuse for Treason.
2 St. Tr. 337.

17. It was resolved by the Court, that if a Paper containing treasonable matter, be indicted by another, yet being known by *Coke* to contain treasonable matter, and being delivered by him as a Charge against the King to take away his Life, this is an Overt Act to prove that he compassed the King's Death, which is the Treason he is Indicted for.

Approbation in High-Treason maketh guilty.
1 H.P.C. 127.

18. And in the Case of High Treason, If any one do any thing by which he shewed his liking and Approbation to the Traiterous Design, this is in him High-Treason: For all are Principals in High Treason, who contribute towards it by Action or Approbation.

19. And

19. And it was resolved that tho' in case a Man be in dicted only for Words, that is not High-Treason. But if a Man be indicted for compassing the King's Death, there Words may be laid as an Overt Act to prove that he compassed the Death of the King, as it was in the Case of *Crohagan*, who being beyond Sea, spake these Words, *I will kill the King, if I can come at him;* and afterwards he came to *England*, and was taken and indicted for compassing the King's Death, and these Words laid as an Overt Act, and proved *, and he had Judgment of High-Treason. And *Co. Pl. Cor.* 14. agreeth, that Words set down in writing, are an Overt Act to prove the compassing the King's Death, as in the Case of Cardinal *Poole* there cited, and Words spoken are the same thing if they be proved; and Words are the natural way for a Man whereby to express the Imagination of the Heart. If it be any way declared that a Man imagineth the King's Death, that is the Treason within the *Stat.* 25 *Edw.* 3. †

Words are an Overt Act to prove Treason. 1 Hawk. 57. & in notis. 1 H.P.C. 127. Cro. Car. p. 332. Fost. 202. Though Co. Pl. Cor. 14. be against this Opinion, yet it was agreed that was no Law. Yet, *Quære*, because of the different Opinions; but Words will explain the meaning of an Act.

20. *Memorandum*, That upon the Tryal of one *Axtell*, a Soldier, who commanded the Guards at the King's Tryal, and at his Murder; he justified that all he did was as his Superiour, no excuse for Treason.

Acting as a Soldier by command of

---

* From this Case thus cited and the Rule that is grounded on it, a Reader would be induced to conclude that the *Words* were the *only* Overt Act laid in the Indictment; but that is not the Case, for besides the Words, the Indictment further charged *that he came into England for the Purpose of killing the King*. Foster's Crown Law, 203. 1 Hal. 116.

† Kelyng seeth no difference between Words *spoken and written*, which is this seditious *Writings* are permanent Things, and if published, they scatter the Poison far and wide, they are Acts of Deliberation capable of Proof, not liable to Misconstruction, but are naked and undisguised as they came out of the Author's Hand: *Words* are transient, and fleeting as the Wind, the Poison they scatter, confined to a narrow Circle of a few Hearers, they are frequently the Effect of sudden Passion, easily misunderstood and often misrepresented. Foster's Crown Law, p. 204. And it has been laid down on more Occasions than one since the Revolution, that loose Words not relative to any Act or Design, are not Overt Acts of Treason. 4 St. Tr. 581, 645. 1 Black. Rep. 37. 1 Hawk. 58, in notis. Whether Words only spoken, can amount to an Overt Act of compassing the King's Death, is very well discussed in H. P. C. from 111 to 120, and 312 to 322; and in Foster's C. L. 195 to 207; who both conclude against the above Assertion of Kelyng.—Hawkins, however, had doubts on the Subject. 1 Hawk. 60. & in notis.

High-Treason.

That otherwise was indifferent.
2 St. Tr. 365
1 Hawk. 54.
in notis.

as a Soldier, by the command of his superiour Officer, whom he must obey or die. It was resolved that was no excuse; for his Superiour was a Traitor, and all that joyned him in that *Act* were Traitors, and did by that approve the Treason; and where the command is Traiterous, there the Obedience to that Command is also Traiterous.

Backstead, Okey, and Corbett's Case.
2 H. P. C. 40.
Foll. 41.
1 Sid. 72.
1 Lev. 61.
2 Keb. 244.
1 Hawk. 3.
in notis.
Foll. 111.
8 S. T. 563.
Execution awarded upon attainder by Outlawry.
Immediate Tryal upon Plea that the Prisoners were not the same Persons.

Memorandum, That in *Easter Term,* 14 *Car.* 2d. *John Barksted, John Okey,* and *Miles Corbet,* three of those Persons who presumed to Judge the late King to Death were apprehended; they then being outlawed upon the former Indictment; and they were brought to the King's Bench Bar, and demanded severally what they could say why Execution should not be awarded against them (after the Indictment was first read to them) and they pleaded they were not the same Persons, and thereupon the same Day a Jury was presently returned, the Court sitting; and they found they were the same Persons, and so execution awarded, which was after done accordingly. *Note, So is the Report in the* Manuscript, *but the Record is of an Attainder by Act of Parliament; but there might be an Outlawry also.*

(14)

Sir Hen. Vane's Case.
2 St. Tr 435.
1 Hawk. 51.
2 Hawk. 615.

The Acts laid were Acts done after the death of King *Ch.* the first, and before the actual restoring of King *Ch.* the second.
1 Hawk. 56.

Memorandum, That in *Trinity Term,* 14 *Car.* 2. Sir *Hen. Vane* was indicted at the King's Bench for compassing the Death of King *Charles* the 2d, and intending to change the Kingly Government of this Nation; and the Overt *Acts* which were laid, were, that he with divers others unknown Persons did meet and consult of the means to destroy the King and Government; and did take upon him the Government of the Forces of this Nation by Sea and Land, and appointed Colonels, Captains, and Officers, and the sooner to effect his wicked Design, did actually in the County of *Middlesex* raise War. And upon his Tryal, he justified that what he did was by the Authority of Parliament, and that the King was then out of Possession of the Kingdom; and the Parliament was the only Power regnant; and therefore, no Treason could be committed against the King: And he objected, that a levying War in *Surrey* could not be given in Evidence to a Jury in *Middlesex;* and he desired to offer a Bill of Exception, because these things were overruled

by

High-Treason.

by the Court; and in this Cafe thefe Points were refolved by the Court.

1. That by the Death of King *Charles* the 1*ſt*, that long Parliament was actually determined; notwithſtanding the *Acts of Parliament* that it ſhould not be diſſolved, but by the confent of both Houſes. For every Parliament is called to confult with the Perſon of the King who calleth it; and therefore upon his Death it is determined; for they can no longer confult with him for which end they were called. And a Cafe was cited to be refolved, that, where, in the 13 of *Q. Eliz.* an *Act of Parliament* was made, that a Commiſſion of *Sewers* ſhould continue for Ten Years, unleſs the fame be determined or repealed by any new Commiſſion, or by *Superdeas*, King *James* granted fuch a Commiſſion and died within that time; Adjudged, that the Commiſſion was determined; for all Commiſſioners are determined by the Death of the *King* who grants them, and this point of the actual determination of that Parliament by the Death of *King Charles* the 1*ſt*, was before that time refolved by all the Judges of *England*, as my Lord *Bridgeman* told me. *But note, there were no ſpecial Words to continue the Parliament upon the King's Death.* [Long Parliament diſſolved by Death of the King. 1 Hawk. 53.]

2. It was refolved, that tho' *King Charles* the 2*d*. was *de facto* kept out of the exerciſe of the Kingly Office by Traitors and Rebels; yet he was *King* both *de facto* & *de Jure*. And all the *Acts* which were done to the keeping him out were High-Treaſon. [Traitors keep out the King, yet Traitors againſt him. 1 Hawk. 51.]

3. It was refolved that the very Confultation and Adviſing together of the means to deſtroy the *King* and his Government, was an Overt *Act* to prove the Compaſſing of the *King's* Death. [Conſulting to deſtroy the King is an Overt Act to prove the Treaſon of compaſſing his Death.]

4. It was refolved that in this Cafe, the Treaſon laid in the Indictment being the Compaſſing of the King's Death, which was in the County of *Middleſex*, and the levying War being laid only as one of the Overt *Acts* to prove the compaſſing of the King's Death, tho' this levying of War be laid in the Indictment to be in *Middleſex*, yet a War levied by him in *Surrey*, might be given in evidence; for being not laid as the Treaſon, but only as the Overt *Act* to prove the compaſſing, it is a tranſitory thing which may be proved in another Country. But if an Indictment be for levying War, and that made the Treaſon for

High-Treason.

for which the Party is indicted, in that Case it is loca., and must be laid in the County where in truth it was.

No Bill of Exception in criminal Causes.
2 Hawk. 602.
1 Sid. 83.
1 Keb. 384.
1 Lev. 68.
2 Inst. 427.

5. It was resolved, that the *Stat. of W.* 2. *Cap.* 31. which giveth the Bill of Exception, extends only to civil Causes, and not to criminal; the Words of the *Stat.* are, *Cum aliquis implacitatur coram aliquibus Justiciariis, &c.* And the Intention never was to give such Persons liberty to put in Bills of Exception, for then there would be no Tryals of that Nature ever discharged in any time, neither here nor in the Circuits, if every frivolous Exception which a Prisoner would make, should be drawn up in a Bill of Exception; besides, the Court is always so far of Counsel with the Prisoner as to see that he hath right, and if they find any thing doubtful, they of themselves will take time to advise: But the Words of the *Stat.* are plain, as the Court agreed, as to this point.

Treason found by the Jury to be several Years before the time in the Indictment.
2 Hawk. 614.

6. Altho' the Treason of compassing the King's Death was laid in the Indictment to be the 30*th* of *May*, 11 *Car.* 2. yet upon the Evidence it appeared, that Sir *Hen. Vane*, the very Day the late *King* was murdered, did sit in Council for the ordering of the Forces of the Nation against the *King* that now is, and so continued on all along until a little before the *King's* coming in. It was resolved that the Day laid in the Indictment is not material, and the Jury are not bound to find him guilty that Day, but may find the Treason to be as it was in truth either before or after the time laid in the Indictment; as it is resolved in *Syer's* Case, *Co. Pl. Coron'* 230. And according in this Case the Jury found Sir *Hen. Vane* guilty of the Treason in the Indictment the 30*th* of *January*, 1 *Car.* 2. which was from the very Day the late *King* was murdered, and so all his forfeitures relate to that time to avoid all conveyances and settlements made by him *.

More than 24 may be returned for criminal Causes.
2 St. Tr. 435.

7. *Memorandum*, That in this Case of Sir *Hen. Vane*, he being to be tryed at the King's Bench Bar, before he came to his Tryal, it was considered by myself, and others then of the King's Council, that it was possible that he might challenge peremptorily, and so defeat his Tryal at that Day, at which it was appointed, if there should be only 24 Jurors returned.

And

---

* Confirmed by all the Judges to be Law. Lord *Balmerino's* Case. Fost. 9. 9 H. Tr. 588. 3 Inst. 230. 1 Hale 361. 2 Hale 179, 291.

High-Treason.

And thereupon, search was made in the Crown Office, and it did appear, that in Tryals on the Crown side for Criminals, the Sheriff might be commanded to return any number the Court pleased; and accordingly, at his Tryal the Sheriff returned about 60 of the Jury; and at common Law in Civil Causes, it seems the Sheriff might have returned above 24 if he pleased; And therefore by the *Stat. W. 2. Cap. 38.* It is recited, that whereas the Sheriffs were used to summon an unreasonable multitude of Jurors to the grievance of the People; it is ordained that from thenceforth, in one Assize, no more shall be summoned than 24, which *Stat.* extends not to Jurors returned for tryal of criminal Persons; the like may be done upon a Commission of *Oyer* and *Terminer*. *For before that Stat. of W. 2. Cap. 38. more than 24 might be returned in civil Causes which is outed by that Stat. five in great Assize, and that Stat. does not extend to criminal Causes or Indictments for the King.*

Memorandum, That at the Sessions at *Newgate*, 11. Dec. 14 Car. 2. *Tho. Thong, Geo. Philips, Francis Stubbs,* and several others, were indicted for High-Treason, for compassing the King's Death, and the Overt Acts laid in the Indictment, were assembling themselves together, and consulting and agreeing to destroy the King. *Ac ad easdem proditiones perimplendas,* the consulting to seize *Whitehall,* where the King was Resident. *Tong's Case. 2 St. Tr. 478. 1 Hawk. 51. in notis 119.*

1. And in this case, It was resolved by all the Judges, that the meeting together of Persons, and consulting to destroy the King, was of itself an Overt Act to prove the compassing the King's Death. *Consulting is an Overt Act. 1 Hawk. 56. Post. 195.*

2. It was resolved that where a Person knowing of the Design does meet with them, and hear them discourse of their traiterous Designs, and say or act nothing; This is High-Treason in that Party, for it is more than a bare Concealment, which is *Misprision,* because it sheweth his liking, and approving of their Design; but if a Person not knowing of their Design before, come into their Company, and hear their Discourses, and say nothing, and never meet with them again at their Consultations, that Concealment is only Misprision of High-Treason. But if he after meet with them again, and hear of their Consultations, and then conceal it, this is High-Treason, For it sheweth a liking, and an approving of their Design; and so was Sir *Everard Digby's* Case, who in the Powder Treason met with the Traitors, and heard their Design, but upon the Evidence it was not proved that he said *Concealment, where it is High-Treason, and where but Misprision. 1 Hawk. 51. in notis. Post 20. 1 Hawk. 86. 1 St. Tr. 224.*

D

High-Treason.

said any Thing, or acted any Thing, and he had Judgment of High-Treason.

Persons in the same Treason, good Witnesses.
2 Hawk. 608. 9.
But see Note to Hawk: on that Passage.
1 H.P.C. 303, 4.

3. It was resolved that some of those Persons who are equally culpable with the rest, may be made use of as Witnesses against their Fellows, and they are lawful Accusers, or lawful Witnesses within the *Stat.* 1 *Ed.* 6. 12. 5 & 6 *Ed* 6. *Cap.* 11. & 1 *Mar.* 1. and accordingly, at the Tryal of these men, some of their Partners in the Treason were made use of against the rest; for lawful Witnesses within those Statutes are such as the Law alloweth; and the Law alloweth every one to be a Witness who is not convicted, or made infamous for some Crime. And if it were not so, all Treasons would be safe; and it would be impossible for one who conspires with never so many others to make a discovery to any purpose.

But the *L. C.* Baron *Hales* said, that if one of these culpable Persons be promised his Pardon, on Condition to give Evidence against the rest, that disableth him to be a Witness against the others, because he is bribed by saving his Life to be a Witness, so that he takes a difference where the Promise of Pardon is to him for disclosing the Treason, and where it is for giving of Evidence*. But some of the other Judges did not think the promise of Pardon, if he gave Evidence, did disable him, but they all advised that no such promise should be made, or any threatnings used to them in case they did not give full Evidence.

Diversity of Opinions.
2 Hawk. 611.

There needs 2 Witnesses for a Treason, at this Day, Stat. 1 & 2 P & M. Cap 10. See afterwards in this Book, fo. 49. more of this Point. Same Witnesses to find the Indictment, and at Tryal.

4. Altho' the Lord Chief Justice *Bridgeman*, and some others of the Judges were of Opinion that those Words of two Witnesses in case of High-Treason, were repealed by the *Stat.* & 2 *Ph.* & *M. Cap.* 10. which enacts that all Tryals for Treason be according to the Course of the Common Law: And at Common Law, one Witness is sufficient to a Jury, tho' *Co. Pl. Cor.* is against this Opinion, yet they all agreed that if that Law for two Witnesses be in force, yet the same two Witnesses who are to the Indictment, may be also the Witnesses at the Tryal: And the Law doth not require two to the finding the Indictment, and two others at the Tryal.

5. They

* The Judges who dissented were Lord Hale and Mr. J. Brown; and Lord Hale is of the same Opinion in 2 H. P. C. 280: But the Opinion of the Majority of the Judges has been ruled to be Law, in Layer's Case. 6 St. Tr. 259, as well as in the present Case; yet for the Reasons in 1 H. P. C. 304, it is a great Objection to the Credibility if not to the Competence of the Witness.

High-Treason.

5. They all agreed that if a Conspirator be examined before a Privy Councellor or a Justice of Peace, and upon his Examination without Torture confess the Treason; If after at his Tryal he deny it, and two Witnesses to prove that Confession, are good Evidence against him that made that Confession, at his Examination aforesaid; and in that case there needs no Witnesses to prove him guilty of the Treason; for that Confession puts it out of the Statute which requires two Witnesses to prove the Treason, unless the Party shall without Torture confess the same; and the Confession there spoken of, is not meant a Confession before the Judges at his Tryal, but a Confession upon his Examination: But such Confession so proved is only Evidence against the Party himself who made the Confession, but cannot be made use of as Evidence against any others whom on his Examination be confessed to be in the Treason.

Confession upon Examination proved by two Witnesses good Evidence of itself.
2 Hawk. 365, 604.
2 H.P.C. 256.
Fost. 240.

6. They all agreed that such a Confession upon Examination before a Privy Councellor, tho' he be not a Justice of Peace, is a Confession within the meaning of the Statute; and the rather Lord *Bridgeman* said, because Justices of the Peace were not enabled to take Examination before the *Stat.* 1 & 2 *P.* & *M. Cap.* 13.

Confession before a Privy Councellor, is a Confession within the Stat.

Memorandum, That a Week before *Christmas*, 15 *Car.* 2. my Brother *Turner,* myself, and my Brother *Archer,* were appointed by the King to go to *York,* for the Tryal of several Persons there taken for conspiring to levy War against the King, and some of them did actually meet in *Farmeleigh-wood* near unto *Leeds,* with Horses, Arms, and Foot Soldiers. And thereupon there was a meeting by the two Chief Justices, my Lord *Hyde,* and my Lord *Bridgeman;* and we three with Sir *Jeff. Palmer* the King's Attorney, and Sir *Heneage Finch* the King's Solicitor, did thereupon debate several Things which were agreed by us all, *viz.*

The North rising Car 15. 2.

1. That if several Persons do agree to levy War, and some of them do actually appear in Arms, and others do not, this is an actual levying of War in all of them, as well those who were not in Arms, as those who were, if they be proved to be of the Plot with them who did actually appear in Arms; for there are no Accessaries in Treason, and therefore all that are in the Conspiracy are equally guilty.

Several Persons agree to raise War, and some appear actually in Arms.
1 H.P.C. 133:
3 Inst. 9, 10.

High-Treason.

1 Hawk. 55.

In the next place, we being informed that tho' there was a Conspiracy to raise War in the *North Riding* of *Yorkshire*, as well as the *West Riding* where some did actually appear in Arms, yet it could not be proved that those in the *North Riding* did agree to the rising that was in the *West Riding*, or that they knew any thing of it, and so would not be within the first Resolution.

New Statute for Safety of the King's Person.

And thereupon the new Statute made the 13 *Car.* 2. for the safety of the King's Person, which maketh the Conspiracy compassing and intending to raise War to be High-Treason, in case they express or declare such Imaginations, Intentions, *&c.* by Printing, Writing, Preaching, or malicious, and advised speaking; and upon that Act it was agreed,

(20)

This Act expired on the Death of C. 2.
Post. 223.
A similar Act had passed in 13 Eliz. and expired at r Death.
1 Hawk. 50, 51, in notis 55, 56.
Post. 220.

2. That if one be indicted for imagining or intending to levy War, there must be some Overt Act laid in the Indictment to prove such Imagination, as there is at this Day in Indictments for compassing and imagining the King's Death; and it was conceived that no Overt Act could be laid to make it Treason within that Statute, but one of those which are named in that Statute, *viz.* Printing, Writing, Preaching, or Malitious, and advised speaking, and we were informed that no Printing, Writing, or Preaching could be proved, and it would be impossible to lay such Words as could be fastened on them, and to prove that they spoke them; but in general we were informed, that their consulting and meeting together, and agreeing to raise War would be proved; and thereupon it was resolved that the best and safest way to proceed against them, was to indict them for compassing and imagining the Death of the King, and to lay the meeting, consulting, and agreeing to levy War, as one Overt Act, and the actual levying War as another Overt Act, and so proceed upon the *Stat.* 25 *Ed.* 3.

Consulting to levy War, is an Overt Act to prove compassing the King's Death.
2 St. Tr. 474.
St. Tr. 435.

3. For it was resolved, and agreed by all now as it was before it was in *Tong*'s Case, and Sir *H. Vane*'s Case, that the meeting and consulting to levy War is an Overt Act to prove the compassing the King's Death within the *Stat.* of *Ed.* 3. Altho' the consulting to levy War is not actual levying within the Statute, and so cannot be indicted thereupon, for that Treason of levying War. Yet if they be indicted for the Treason of compassing and imagining the King's Death, that consulting to levy War is

an

High-Treason.

an Overt Act to prove that Treason, altho' *Co. Pl. Cor.* 14. delivers an Opinion against this.

4. It was resolved, that if Persons do actually levy War, so that they may be indicted for the Treason of levying of War, within the *Stat.* 25 *Ed.* 3. Yet they may be indicted for compassing the King's Death, and their actual levying of War may be laid as an Overt Act to prove the compassing the King's Death: And tho' *Co. Pl. Cor.* 14. be of another Opinion, yet that is no Law: For he expresly contradicts himself, for he reports the Case of the Lord *Copham*, 1 *Jacobi* 1.

(21) Actual War an Overt Act to prove the compassing the King's Death. Dyer 308. Pl. 73.

And the Case of the Earl of *Essex*, 43 *Eliz.* where it was resolved by all the Judges, That the gathering of Men together to compel the King to yield to certain Demands, or to remove ill Councellors, was an Overt Act to prove the compassing of the King's Death, for which they were indicted, so *Co. Pl. Cor.* 12. accords, and in the same Book, *Fo.* 14, &c. agreeth, That if a Subject conspire with a Foreign Prince beyond Seas to invade the Realm, and prepare for the same by some Overt Act, this is a sufficient Overt Act to prove him guilty of Treason in compassing the King's Death. And it was observed that in these Posthumous Works of Sir *E. Coke*, of the Pleas of the Crown, and Jurisdiction of Courts, many great Errors were published, and in particular in his discourse of Treason, and in the Treatise of Parliaments.

1 St. Tr. 307.

Errors in *Co. Pl. cor.* Jurisdiction of Courts, of Treason, and of Parliaments.

5. It was agreed that the bare knowledge of Treason, and the concealment of it was not High-Treason, but Misprision of Treason. But in Case any thing be proved upon Evidence, that the Party liked or approved of it, then it is High-Treason; or if the Party knew of the Design, and after such Knowledge, met with the Conspirators at their Consultation; or if he went knowingly to their Consultations several Times, this is Evidence of his Approbation of the Design, and is High-Treason.

Misprision of Treason; what, and what not. Ante 17. 1 Hawk. 86. 4 Black. Com. 120.

6. It was agreed that to make a Misprision of Treason, there must be a Knowledge of the Design, and of the Persons, or some of them; for a Man cannot be said to conceal what he doth not know; and therefore, if one tell

What requisite to make Misprision of Treason.

Hawk. 87. tell *I. S.* in general, that there will be a rising without acquainting him with the Persons who are to rise, or with the Nature of the Plot, If *I. S.* conceal this, this is no Misprision of Treason, because he hath no Knowledge of the Treason.

Misprision what is a discovery, and what not. 1 Hawk. 87.

7. It was agreed that if one knew of a Treason, and knew some of the Conspirators, and then tell other Men in general Terms that there will be a rising, &c. without a discovery of the Plot, or the Traitors, such a Discourse will not acquit him from Misprision of Treason by concealment of it, because notwithstanding those general Discourses, both the Treason and the Traitors are concealed by him.

What shall be a discovery of Treason.

8. And in case such a Person who knoweth of a Treason, and the Traitors, and discovers all he knoweth to another Person who is not a Privy Councellor, or a Justice of Peace, or hath Authority to take Examinations concerning it, it was doubted whether such a discovery would acquit him from concealing of Treason which is Misprision.

Twyn's Case. 2 St. T. 528. 8 St. 380. 1 Hawk. 51, 56. Printing Treasonable Positions, an Overt Act to make good an Indictment, for compassing the King's Death.

At the Sessions in the *Old Bailey,* 20 *Feb.* 15 *Car.* 2. *John Twyn* was indicted on the *Stat.* 25 *Ed.* 3. of High-Treason, for compassing and imagining the King's Death, and the Overt Act laid in the Indictment was, the Printing of a Seditious, Poisonous and Scandalous Book, entituled, *A Treatise of the Execution of Justice, wherein is clearly proved that the Execution of Judgment and Justice is as well the Peoples as the Magistrates Duty, and if the Magistrates pervert Judgment, the People are bound by the Law of God to execute Judgment without them.* And besides that Title of the Book, several Passages in the Book were set forth in the Indictment, which in substance were, first, That the supreme Magistrate is accountable to the People. 2. The People are incited to take the Management of the Government into their own Hands. 3. The People are encouraged to take up Arms against the King and his Family. 4. They are stirred up to revolt, as an Action honourable and conscientious, and Encouragements

ments given to any Town, City or County in the three Kingdoms to begin the Work. 5. The People are exhorted, not only to caſt off their Allegiance, but to put the King to Death. And upon the Evidence it was proved, that *Twyn* being a Printer, by himſelf and Servants printed this Book; That he corrected ſome of the Sheets, and that he ſcattered many of them to be ſold; and he was found guilty, and had Judgment for High-Treaſon, and was accordingly executed.

At this Tryal were preſent of the Judges the Chief Juſtice *Hyde*, and myſelf, and alſo my Brother *Wylde* Recorder of *London*, and reſolved by all clearly, That Printing and Publiſhing ſuch wicked Poſitions, was an Overt Act declaring the Treaſon of compaſſing and imagining the King's Death, which was alſo agreed by the Reſt of the Judges upon our Diſcourſe with them. At the ſame Seſſions *Simon Dover*, *Tho. Brewſter*, and *Nathan Brookes*, Printers and Bookſellers, were indicted at the Common Law, as for a great Miſdemeanour for printing and publiſhing one Book, called, *The Speeches and Prayers of Harriſon, Cook, Hugh Peters*, and others condemned for the Murder of the late King, in which were many deſperate Paſſages, juſtifying their Villainy; and another Book called, *The Phœnix, or Solemn League and Covenant*; In which alſo were Paſſages of dangerous Conſequence. And they being found guilty, it was reſolved, That tho' Printing be a Trade, and ſelling of Books alſo, yet they muſt uſe their Trade according to Law, and not abuſe it, by printing or ſelling of Books ſcandalous to the Government, or tending to Sedition. So in caſe of a Councellor at Law, he may plead his Clyent's Cauſe againſt the King; but if, under Colour of that, he takes upon him to vent Sedition, he is to be puniſhed.

Brewſter and *Brooke's* Caſe. 2 St. Tr. 528, 538, 545.

Memorandum. *Cooke's* Caſe, a Lawyer in *Gray's-Inn*, who managed that villainous Charge againſt the late King at his Tryal, would have excuſed himſelf, becauſe he acted only as Counſel; but that would not ſerve his turn; he was executed with the Reſt. And in this principal Caſe the Perſons were told, that the King had dealt Mercifully

Judgment. 2 St. Tr. 337.

High-Treason.

Judgment against Brewster and others.

Mercifully with them, that he did not proceed against them capitally, and they were all fined, *viz.* *Brewster* 100 Marks, and *Dover* and *Brookes* 40 Marks apiece, and every of them to stand in the *Pillory*, one Day at the *Exchange*, from Eleven to One, and another Day in *Smithfield*, for the same Time, with Papers on their Hats, declaring their Offence for printing and publishing scandalous, treasonable, and factious Books against the King and Government, and to lie in Goal without Bail till the next Goal Delivery, and then to make an open Confession and Acknowledgment of their Offences in such Words as should then be Directed; and afterwards to remain in Prison during the King's Pleasure, and not to be discharged before every one of them put in good Sureties by Recognizance, themselves in 400*l.* apiece, and two Sureties for each of them in 200*l.* apiece, not to Print or Publish any Books but such as shall be allowed by Authority.

Newgate Sessions, 14 *October,* 14 *Car.* 2.

Raven's Case.
1 Hawk. 134, 137.

Co. Pl. Cor. 107, 108.
1 Hawk. 546, 7.

Mary Raven, alias *Aston,* was indicted for stealing two Blankets, three pair of Sheets, three Pillowbiers, and other Goods of *William Cannon.* And upon the Evidence it appeared, that she had hired Lodgings and Furniture with them for three Months, and during that Time, conveyed away the Goods which she had hired with her Lodgings, and she herself ran away at the same Time *. And it was agreed by my Lord *Bridgeman,* myself, and my Brother *Wylde,* Recorder of *London,* then present, that this was no Felony, because she had a special Property in them by her Contract, and so there could be no Trespass; and there can be no Felony where there is no Trespass, as it was resolved in the Case of *Holmes,* who set fire on his own House in *London,* which was quenched before it went further. *Vide* the End of this Book, *Kelyng contra* 81.

2 Hawk. 546, 7.

At the same Sessions one was indicted for Murder, and upon his Tryal was found guilty of Manslaughter, and then offered to plead the King's Pardon, which upon sight of it *pardon' feloniam & felonicam interfecćon'* of the Man slain, *Non obstant'* the *Stat.* of 10 *E.* 3. & 13 *R.* 2. which

was

---

* Altered by Stat. 3, 4. W. & M. 2, 9. Vide Postea 81. Denied to be Law, and found Felony.

was agreed by us all to be a Pardon of Murder, notwithstanding the Proceedings in *Rickabee*'s Cafe by *Rolls* during the late Troubles, and then the Queſtion was, if now the Party had not loſt the Benefit of his Pardon; for he that pleads a Pardon confeſſeth the Fact, and relyeth upon the King's Mercy: And therefore, if after his Pardon, he plead not guilty, he waved his Pardon, which is clear Law *. But here the Queſtion was, becauſe this Pardon here by the expreſs Words pardons Man-ſlaughter only, and then by reaſon of the *non obſtant* it extends to pardon Murder, whether tho' he waved it as to Murder, he might not make uſe of it as to Man-ſlaughter. And as to that, there being ſome difference in Opinion, the Party was bailed, and had a Certificate from us of the Nature of the Caſe, and thereupon obtained a new Pardon. But it was agreed by us all, if the Pardon had not extended to pardon Murder, he could not poſſibly make uſe of it. And therefore, upon this Tryal, he was only found guilty of Man-ſlaughter, he might plead that Pardon, and it ſhould have been allowed: And after, when he came to plead his new Pardon, and that was allowed, he paid Gloves to the Judges, which is a due Fee for that, *Vide* 4 *E*. 4. 10 *B. Pulton de pace* 88. *a*.

March 213.
Styles 369.
2 Hawk. 549, 42, 3.
Wilſon 150.
Hale 252.
S. P. C. 173, 169.
B. Cor. 200.

Gloves due to Judges on allowance of Pardons.
2 Hawk. 562.

Memorandum, In the aforeſaid Caſe it was moved, that the Court ſhould not abſolutely diſcharge the Perſon, but ought to commit him or bail him, until the Year and a Day after the Fact committed, by the Statute of 3 *H.* 7. *C.* 1. But upon ſight of that Statute it appeared that that Statute extends only where Perſons are indicted for Murder, and are acquitted, there they are to be committed or bailed till the Year and a Day paſt, that if any one will bring an Appeal, he may be forth-coming: But extends not to Perſons who being indicted for Murder are found guilty of Man-ſlaughter, or *ſe defendendo*, or by miſchance.

Stat. 3 H. 7. for committing or bailing extends only to ſuch as are acquitted for Murder, and to ſuch as are found guilty of Man-ſlaughter.

At the ſame Seſſions, one *John Roberts* was indicted as a Principal in a Burglary, and upon the Evidence it appeared, that he was only acceſſary after the Fact, by be arraigned as Acceſſary before the Fact, but he may be arraigned again as Acceſſary after the Fact.

One acquitted of the principal Fact cannot after

* But ſee the King and Haines Wils. 214. where the Benefit of an Act of Grace was allowed after the general Iſſue pleaded.

receiving those who did it, and the Goods, and thereupon it was doubted, that if the Jury should acquit him, as they must upon this Indictment, whether he might afterwards be indicted as Accessary. And therefore to avoid all doubt, the Court discharged the Jury of him, and ordered another Indictment to be against him as Accessary. But afterwards, upon Consideration of the Books, we did agree, that the Law was, If one was indicted as Principal and acquitted, he cannot after be indicted as Accessary before the Fact: But notwithstanding such Acquittal, he may be indicted as accessary after the Fact, and the Reason is, because he that commands or advises a Robbery, Burglary, or Murder to be committed is *quodam modo* guilty of the Fact; And therefore if he be found not guilty of the Fact, being indicted as Principal, he cannot afterwards be tried as Accessary before the Fact, because by the former Verdict, he is found not to be guilty of the Fact, which extends to all guilt before the principal Fact committed. But an Accessary after is not guilty in any sort of committing the Fact, for it was done before he knew any thing of it; therefore if he be tried as Principal, and found not guilty, he may be after indicted as Accessary after; for that is an Offence subsequent to the committing of the Fact, and is for receiving the Felons, or after the Fact done, which is an Offence of another Nature: So are the Books, 27 *Ass. Pl.* 10. 8 *H.* 5, 6, 7. And so have the Presidents upon Examination always been at *Newgate* Sessions.

Accessary before or after, Diversity as to acquital on Indictment as Principal. 2 Hawk. 529. S.P.C. 44, 105. Sum. 224, 244. 1 Hale 626. Foster 362. Post. 30, 47, 52. Post. 30, contra. See the Case of Samuel Atkyns. 2 St. Tr. 783.

At the same Sessions, *Edward Rew* was indicted for killing *Nathaniel Rew* his Brother, and upon the Evidence, it was resolved, that if one gives Wounds to another, who neglects the Cure of them, or is disorderly, and doth not keep that Rule which a Person wounded should do; yet if he die it is Murder or Manslaughter, according as the Case is in the Person who gave the Wounds, because if the Wounds had not been, the Man had not died; and therefore neglect or disorder in the Person who received the Wounds, shall not excuse the Person who gave them.

Rew's Case. Disorder or neglect, not excuse the Person who gave the Wounds. 1 Hawk. 119.

At

At the fame Seffions, *Thomas Middleton*, Tooth-drawer on *Ludgate-hill*, was indicted for marrying two Wives, and upon his Tryal, he produced a Sentence of Divorce from his firft Wife under Seal *Caufa Adulterij*, of her Part, and agreed that he was not within that Statute, for *Rooke's* Cafe was ftronger, which fee, 1 *Cro.* 461. where the Divorce was *caufa fevitiæ*, and that adjudged to excufe from the Statute.

Middleton's Cafe. Two Wives and Party Divorced *caufa Adulterij* not within Stat. 21 *Jacob*. *Sed Vide* Duchefs of *Kingfton's* H. P. C. 694.

Cafe. 11 St. Tr. 198. 1 Hawk. 174.

At the fame Seffions, one *Henry Burgefs* was indicted for breaking up a Chamber in *Somerfet-houfe*, and the Indictment laid it to be *dom' Manconal'* of the Perfon who lodged in it. And it was agreed, that the Indictment was not good, becaufe all *Somerfet-houfe* is one intire Houfe of the *Queen-mother*, and all who Lodge in it are her Servants; and therefore it ought to be *dom' Manconal'* of the *Queen-mother*. So for *White-hall*, which is the King's Houfe; and it differs from the Cafe of an Inns of Court, where every Gentleman hath a feveral Intereft, and therefore there every feveral Chamber is *domus Manconal'* of the Perfon who hath the Intereft.

Burgefs's Cafe. Chamber in *Sommerfet-houfe*, not the Manfion-Houfe of him who abideth in it; otherwife of a Chamber in Inns of Court. 1 Hawk. 162. 2 Hawk. 500. See Foff. 39. 1 H.P.C. 527.

557. 2 Hawk. 499. Sum. 237, 8. *Lee v. Ganfel Cowper* 1. 2 Salk. 552.

At the fame Seffions, one *John Legg*, being indicted for the Murder of Mr. *Robert Wife*. It was upon the Evidence agreed, that if one Man kill another, and no fudden Quarrel appeareth, this is Muder, as *Co.* 9. *Rep. fol.* 67. *b*. *Makelly's* Cafe. And it lyeth upon the Party indicted to prove the fuddain Quarrel.

Legg's Cafe. Murder to kill one without Caufe, the fuddain Quarrel lyeth in the Prifoner to prove. 1 Hawk. 124.

And in this Cafe it was alfo agreed, that if two Men fall out in the Morning, and meet and Fight in the Afternoon, and one of them is flain, this is Murder, for there was time to allay the Heat, and their after-meeting is of Malice.

Quarrel in Morning, Fight in Afternoon, Murder.

1 Hawk. 122, 123. Foft. 27.

At the fame Seffions, *George Thorley*, being indicted for Robbery, refufed to plead, and his two Thumbs were tyed together with Whipcord, that the Pain of that might compel him to plead, and he was fent away fo tyed, and a Minifter perfwaded to go to him to perfwade him; And an Hour after he was brought again and pleaded.

Thorely's Cafe. One ftand Mute, Thumbs tyed together with Whipcord. 2 H.P.C. 319.

2 Hawk. 467. pleaded. And this was said to be the conſtant Practice at *Newgate* *.

What Circumſtances inquirable where one kills another in keeping the Peace, or where a Parent or Maſter kills a Child or Servant in chaſtizing.
1 Hawk. 105.
2 Roll. 120.
Sum. 38.

Note, That although if an Officer or other Perſon kill another in preſerving the Peace, or a Parent, Maſter, or Schoolmaſter kills his Child, Servant or Scholar in chaſtizing or correcting him, this ſhall be ſaid to be *per Infortunium,* yet *Vide Stat.* 1 *Jac. C.* 8. for ſtabbing, there at the End of it, there is a *proviſo,* that the Statute ſhall not extend to any Perſon who ſhall kill in keeping and preſerving the Peace, ſo as the Man-ſlaughter be not committed wilfully and of purpoſe, under pretext of keeping the Peace; nor to a Maſter or Parent in chaſtizing his Child or Servant, beſides his or their Intent or Purpoſe, ſo that thoſe Circumſtances are inquirable in thoſe Caſes.

Clergy, the Court Judge of reading, not the Ordinary.
2 Hawk. 505, 506.

Vide 9 *E.* 4. 28. One demands his Clergy, and the Court took the Book and turned him to a Verſe, and he could not read well, but read one Word in one Place and another Word in another Place. And the Judges aſked the *Ordinary* if he would have him; and he anſwered yea. The Judges bid him conſider, and told him the Court was Judge of his reading, and if the Court ſhould Judge he did not read, the *Ordinary* ſhould be fined, and the Priſoner hanged, notwithſtanding his demanding of him, and he was hanged, *Vide Fitz Abridgment, titulo Corone* 32. And *Vide* at the End of the Caſe in the Book at Large, *viz.* 9 *E.* 4. 286. ſeveral Books are cited where in the Abſence of the *Ordinary,* the Court delivered the Book to the Priſoner, *Vid* the ſame Book.

In the Abſence of the Ordinary the Court may deliver the Book F.N.B. 66, h. accordingly the Court delivered the Book in abſence of the Ordinary. 2 Hawk. 506, 7.

2 Hale 381. Pardon void, becauſe the King d'd not take notice the Party had abjured.
2 Hawk. 542.

A Man who had abjured the Realm for the Death of a Man, was brought to the Bar, and being demanded what he could ſay, why Execution ſhould not be awarded. He pleaded the King's Pardon, which was diſallowed, becauſe there was no mention in it, that he had abjured; and after he prayed his Clergy, which was diſallowed *ut ſupra;* and after he pleaded, he was taken out of a *Sanctuary,* and deſired to be reſtored, which the Court refuſed, and ſaid he ſhould not have that Plea, becauſe being aſked what he could ſay, why Judgment and Execution

* This Practice is rendered unneceſſary by 12 *Geo.* 3. C. 20.

cution should not be given and awarded against him, he had pleaded his Pardon, and that being disallowed, he should not be received to plead any other Plea, which was ruled accordingly, for he was hanged. So *Note*, Tho' a Prisoner in such a Case, must at his Peril plead such a Plea as he will stand to, for it is peremptory to him if the matter, &c. pleaded be judged against him; yet after such Plea, he may and ought to have the the Benefit of his Clergy.

When a Prisoner is demanded what he can say, why Judgment should not be given, His first Plea is peremptory if that be over-ruled, yet Clergy allowed in that Case after Plea judged against him.

At the Sessions for *Newgate*, 20 *April* 1664. 16 *Car.* 2. The Chief Justice *Hyde*, myself, and Justice *Wylde* present, One *John Joyner* was indicted for stealing a Copper, and upon the Evidence it appeared the Copper was fixed to the Freehold, and he broke it up and carried it away; And thereupon the Jury was directed by the Court, that he was not guilty, because it was no Felony. But my Lord Chief Justice *Hyde* said, that it being so rank a Trespass the Jury might find it Specially, that he did take up the Copper, but that it was fixed, and so leave it to the Court, to judge whether Felony or no, and thereupon the Court judge it Trespass, and fine him, and give him other Punishment fit for such a Trespass, as the Court did in *Holmes*'s Case, *Cro.* I *Part.* 376, 377. But my Brother *Wylde* and I differed in that Point, and said it was not like *Holmes*'s Case; For there all the special Matter was expressed in the Indictment, *viz.* That *Holmes* being possessed of a House in *London*, did *Felonice* set on Fire his own House and burn it with intent to burn the Houses of other Men near adjoining, and of this the Jury found him guilty, and before Judgment, because the Court doubted whether it was Felony or no, the Record was removed into the *King's-Bench*, and the Advice of all the Judges taken, and agreed, that it was no Felony: And thereupon all the special Matter being in the Indictment, and he found guilty of that as it was laid, in Law it being no Felony, he was found guilty of the Trespass, for which the Court gave Judgment against him. But in this Case he is indicted generally for stealing a Copper, which may not be fixed, and if the Jury should find him guilty generally, the Court must give Judgment as for Felony. For the special Matter that it was fixed is not laid in the Indictment. And it would be dishonourable for the Court in so plain a Case as this, to suffer the Jury

Joyner's Case. Whereupon an Indictment for Felony, the Court may give Judgment for Trespass.

1 Jones. 351.
1 Hawk. 166.

Jury to find a special Verdict, so all agreed that the Jury should find him not guilty, which was done accordingly, *Vide* 1 H. 7. 10, *b*. Though Felony includes Trespass, yet if the Party indicted be discharged of the Felony, which is Principal, he is thereby acquitted of the Trespass, *tamen Quære* of this, and *Vide* the Book.

2 Hale 500.
1 Hawk. 625.

Locoft and Villars's Case. Burglary to break an House in the Night with an intent to commit Felony.
1 Hawk. 164.

At the same Sessions *John Locoft* and *Lawrence Villars* were indicted for Burglary for breaking and entering a Man's House with an intent to Ravish his Wife, and were found guilty, and had Judgment to be hanged. Upon the Evidence, the Fact was very foul, for the Woman was actually ravished by one, and afterwards thrust a Torch betwixt her Legs, &c.

Will. Turner's Case.

If one break an House in the Night, steal Goods thence of several Men, and be indicted for that Burglary, and stealing the Goods of one of the Men, and be acquitted, he cannot be afterwards indicted for the Burglary, but may for the Felony, for stealing the Goods of other Men, which were taken out of the same House.
2 Hawk. 527.

At the same Sessions there was this Question, One *James Turner* and *William Turner*, at *Christmas* Sessions last, were indicted of Burglary for breaking the House of Mr. *Tryton* in the Night, and taking away great Sums of Money: and thereupon *James Turner* was found guilty and executed; but *William Turner* was then acquitted. And now there being great Evidence that *William Turner* was in the same Burglary with *James Turner*, and there being 47*l.* of the Money of one *Hill*, a Servant to Mr. *Tryton*, stolen at the same Time, which 47*l.* was not in the former Indictment, they would have indicted *William Turner* again now for Burglary, for breaking the House of Mr. *Tryton*, and taking thence 47*l.* of the Money of *Hills*; but we all agreed that *William Turner* being formerly indicted for Burglary in breaking the House of Mr. *Tryton*, and stealing his Goods, and acquitted, he cannot now be indicted again for the same Burglary for breaking the House; but we all agreed, he might be indicted for Felony, for stealing the Money of *Hill*. For they are several Felonies, and he was indicted of this Felony before, and so he was indicted. And afterwards I told my Lord Chief Justice *Bridgeman* what we had done, and he agreed the Law to be so as we had directed.

At

At the *Lent Assizes* at *Cambridge*. 16 *Car.* 2. *Clement Simson* was indicted for breaking an House in the Day Time, no body being in the House, and stealing Plate to the Value of 10*l.* And upon the Evidence it appeared, that he had taken the Plate out of a Trunk in which it was, and laid it on the Floor; but before he carried it away, he was surprised by People coming into the House. And the Chief Justice *Hyde* caused this to be found Specially, because he doubted upon the *Stat.* of 39 *Eliz. Cap.* 15. That enacts, that if any one be found guilty of the Felonious, taking away any Goods, *&c.* out of any House in the Day-time, above the Value of 5s. he should not have the Benefit of his *Clergy*, Whether this were a taking away within the Statute. And on the 13 *June*, *Car.* 2. All the Judges being met together, this Question was propounded to them, and agreed that *Clergy* was taken away in this Case. For the *Stat.* of 39 *Eliz.* does not go about to declare what shall be Felony, but to take away *Clergy* from that kind of Felony. For breaking an House in the Day-time, no body being therein, and stealing Goods above the Value of five Shillings, so that the Felony is at Common Law; And by the Common Law, breaking the House and taking of Goods, and removing them from one Place to another in the same House, with an intent to steal them is Felony; For by this taking them he hath the Possession of them, and that is Stealing and Felony. *Vide* for this 27 *Aff. Pl.* 39. *Br. Corone* 107

Simson's Case. Removing Goods from one Place in an House to another by a Thief, who intended to steal them is Felony, tho' he be surprized before he carry them away. And if a Thief do so in the Day-time, by breaking an House no body being therein, his Clergy is taken away by Stat. 39 *Eliz.* if the Goods be above the value of 5s. 1 Hawk. 141. 1 H.P.C. 508. 527. 2 H.P.C. 358. Fost. 108. 1 Hawk. 151. in notis.

At the same Time it was propounded to all the Judges If a Man and his Wife go both together to commit a Burglary, and both of them break a House in the Night, and enter and steal Goods; what Offence this was in the Wife, and agreed by all, that it was no Felony in the Wife? for the Wife being together with the Husband in the Act, the Law supposeth the Wife doth it by *coertion* of the Husband, and so it is in all *Larcenies*; but as to Murder, if Husband and Wife doth join in it, they are both equally guilty, *Vide* 2 *E* 3. *F. Corone* 160. 27 *Aff. Pl.* 40. *F. Corone* 199. *Poulton de pace* 126, *b.* And the Case of the Earl of *Summerset* and his Lady, both equally found guilty of the Murder of *Sir Thomas Overbury*, by poysoning him at the *Tower* of *London*.

Husband and Wife commit Larceny or Felony together, no Felony in Wife, but only the Husband is guilty, otherwise in case of Murder both guilty. 1 Hawk. 3, 4. and in notis. 1 St. Tr. 348, 351.

At

Murder and other Offences.

Ann Davis's Case.
1 Hawk. 121.

2 Hawk. 618, 619.
2 Hale 228, 9.

2 H.P.C. 289.

Special Verdict.

At the Goal Delivery for *Newgate*, holden 31 *August*, 16 *Car.* 2. my Lord *Bridgeman*, myself, and my Brother *Wylde*, Recorder of *London*, being present; *Ann Davis* was indicted for murdering her Male Bastard Child, and the Indictment was not special as the Statute is for concealing it, *&c.* But the Indictment was *quod Infantem masculum vivum parturiit qui quidem infans masculus adtunc & ibid. vivus existens natus per legem hujus regni Angl' spurius fuit, Anglice,* a Bastard, and then goeth on in the ordinary Form, that she murdered it, and doth not conclude *Contra formam Statut.* And it was doubted by us, whether the Indictment ought not to be special. And we caused Presidents to be searched, and 2 *Car.* 1. there was a special Indictment, but after 4, 5 & 6 *Car.* 1. All the Indictments were as this is, and Mr. *Lee*, Clerk of the Peace for *London*, said that the Form was altered, and made as it is now by the Advice of the Judges at that Time, who agreed that Clause which is now in the Indictment, should be put in and to conclude generally *contra pacem, &c.* and not to conclude, *contra formam Statut.* For Murder was an Offence at Common Law; and the Statute declareth, that where the Child is concealed, it shall be taken to be born alive, and if it be dead it shall be taken, that it was murdered, and so the Statute doth not make a new Offence, but maketh a Concealment to be an undeniable Evidence that she murdered it; and so the Court was satisfied, and went on upon the Indictment, and upon the Evidence it appeared, that the Prisoner lived in a Chamber by herself, and went to Bed on *Thursday* Night well, without any Pain, and in the middle of the Night waked full of Pain, and knocked for some body to come to her, and one Woman heard her knock, but came not to her, and the same Night she was delivered of a Child, and after she put the Child in a Trunk, and did not discover it till *Friday* Night following, and this was found specially to have the Advice of all the Judges, whether that knocking for help at the Time of her Travel (altho' she concealed it after one Day) exempts her from that Statute. For there was no sign of any Hurt upon the Body of the Child. But thus far it was agreed by us, that if there be an intent in the Woman to conceal the Child, then it is Murder by that Statute, though in truth

truth the Child was dead born. But if there was no Intent to conceal it, or if *she confess herself with Child* before hand, and after she is surprifed and delivered, no body being with her, this is not within the Statute, becaufe there was no intent to conceal it, and therefore in Cafe, if there be no fign of hurt upon the Child, it is no Murder.

If no intent to conceal the Child, not Murder within the Statute. 2 Hawk. 619.

At the fame Seffions *Joseph Clarke* was indicted in *London* for High-Treafon, for Coining of Money, and upon the Evidence it was proved againſt him in *London,* as it ought to be, the Indictment being there, but a great deal of more Evidence was given againſt him of committing the fame Crime in *Middlefex,* and in *Effex,* which was agreed to be good Evidence to fatisfy the Jury.

Joseph Clark's Cafe for coining of Money.

Vide Devant. 15, a.

One *Richard Oliver* who had been partner with him in the Crime, and formerly convicted for that Crime, and had obtained the King's Pardon, was ufed as a Witnefs againſt him, together with other Witneffes. And it was agreed by us all, that the bare uttering of falfe Money, though the Party know it be falfe Money, is not High-Treafon, nor Mifprifion of Treafon; For nothing is Mifprifion of High-Treafon but concealing it, yet the uttering of falfe Money is a great Mifprifion finable, if the Party know it to be falfe: But if he that utters it know the Perfon that coined it, or if one help a Coiner with Inftruments and Tools to coin withal, or furnifh him with Silver for his coining, and Money is coined accordingly, in every of thefe Cafes it is High-Treafon in them who utter the Money, or affift the Coiner with Materials, for they are all aiding to the Treafon; and in High-Treafon, every one who giveth aid or affiftance to it, are Principals; for there are no Acceffaries in Treafon, and they are guilty of Coining as well as he that coined it.

Oliver's Cafe. 2 Hawk. 609, 1 H.P.C. 304, in notis.

1 Hawk. 62.

A Form of Conviction for High Ways, by the View of a Juftice of Peace, which he is to return to the next Seffions, and a Form of an Order thereupon, which I had from my Lord *Hyde.*

Bedford.
1 Hawk. 414.
Sect. 71.

Memorand' quod Un'——Justiciar' Dom' Regis ad pacem in Com. præd. conservand' nec non ad diversas felonias & transgression' & al, malefacta in eod. Com' perpetrat' audiend & terminand' assignat' ad hanc Generalem Sessionem. Pacis Com. præd. tent. apud——infra Com. præd.——die &c. Anno Regni Dom, &c. *coram præfat.——&——Justic. pacis in Com. præd. virtute Statut. Dom. Eliz. nuper Reginæ Angl' in Parliamento tent' apud Westmon'* 12 *die Jan. Anno nuper Reginæ* 5 *& secundum formam & effectum dict. Statut. Intitulat.* An Act for the reviving of a Statute made *An.* 2 *&* 3 *Phil. & Ma.* for the mending of High-ways, *super propriam notitiam suam presentavit qd. Quædam cumunis & Antiqua Regia via infra paroch. præd. in Com præd. quæ ducit de Paroch. præd. ad de——villam in Com. præd. (mercatoriam villa existen.) a quodam loco vocat. in Paroch. præd. usque ad quendam pontem communiter vocat. in Parocha prædict non est bene & sufficient. reperat. & emendat. secundum formam & effect Statut. præd. sed modo est in magno decasu ita quod subditi dic. Dom. Reg. per viam præd cum equis, plaustris, Carrucis & Carriagijs & al' necessarijs suis prout solebant & debent absque magno periculo transire seu laborare non possunt in cujus rei testimonium præd. ——manum & sigillum suum apposuit.*

Ordo super inde.

Super quo ad eandem General' Sessionem pacis ibid' tent. die & anno supradictis, præd. Justiciarij Dom. Regis ad pacem Dict. Dom. Regis in Com. præd. conservand. assig. nat. assessaver. & imposuerunt finem 40l. *levand. de Inhabitantibus dict Paroch. de---in quorum Defect' via pred' non est bene & sufficienter reparat secund. formam Stat. præd. si præd. via non sit sufficienter reparat. & emendat. ante Festum sci' Johannis Baptist. prox. futurum.*

What only is traverſable on this Conviction.
Vide Saunders Reps. 2 *p.* 160.

Memorandum, Upon such a Conviction the decay of the High-way cannot be traversed, but they may plead, that some other Person ought to repair it, and traverse that they ought not, but the decay being upon View of a Justice of Peace cannot be gainsaid or traversed.

This

Murder and other Offences.

This is the best way to have all High-ways amended if the Justices of Peace would do their Duty. My Lord *Hyde* also told me, that it was resolved by all the Judges in *Gaye*'s Case, 2 *Car.* 1. that if a Recusant who was proclaimed at the Assizes according to the Statute, render himself the next Assizes to plead or traverse, &c. he must appear in Person, and he is to be in Custody; for the Words of the Statute and of the Proclamation are, that he shall render his body to the Sheriff of the County.

Gaye's Case. Recusant after Proclamation to appear in Person, and to be in Custody.

At the Sessions in the *Old Bailey* holden there the 12 *October* 1664. A *Silk Throster* had Men come to Work in his own House, and delivered Silk to one of them to Work, and the Workmen stole away part of it. It was agreed by *Hyde* Chief Justice, myself, and Brother *Wylde* being there, that this was Felony, notwithstanding the delivery of it to the Party, for it was delivered to him only to Work, and so the entire Property remained then only in the Owner, like the Case of a *Butler*, who hath Plate delivered to him; or a Shepherd, who hath Sheep delivered, and they steal any of them, that is Felony at the Common Law, *Vide* 13 *Eliz.* 4. 10. 3 *H.* 7. 12. & 11 *H.* 7. 14. *accord. Poulton de pace* 126.

Felony in Goods, notwithstanding the Delivery of them. 1 Hawk. 135. in notis.

At the same Time there being Discourse, about the restitution of Goods stolen, (to the Owner, who had prosecuted the Thief) my Brother *Wylde* said that it had been resolved upon the Words of the *Stat.* of 21 *H.* 8. *Cap.* 11. which giveth restitution of stolen Goods to the Owner in case the Thief be upon his Evidence found Guilty, that notwithstanding a Sale in a Market Overt by the Thief of the Goods stolen; yet the Party shall have Restitution: And he said, so was the Practice at the *Old Bailey*. But my Lord *Hyde* and myself, were of a contrary Opinion, because at Common Law, a Sale in a Market Overt by a Party who hath no Property shall bind the Right of the true Owner, and so is *More Rep.* 360. The Bishop of *Worcester*'s Case, where to a Restitution granted at a Sessions of *Newgate*, the Party who had brought the Goods pleaded a Sale to him in a Market Overt, there the Case was adjudged against the Defendant, because it appeared not to be a Sale in a Market Overt. For it was Plate sold in a Scrivener's Shop in *London*. But there no Question

Restitution of stolen Goods, if grantable to the Prosecutor upon the Statute in case the Goods were sold in a Market Overt. 2 Hawk. 250. 1 H.P.C. 543.

is made, but that a Sale in a Market Overt would have hindered the Restitution, and bound the Property of the right Owner. And by the *Stat.* of 31 *Eliz. Cap.* 12. which in case of Horses stolen, enabled the Owner to have Restitution if he claim them, within six Months after they are sold by the Thief in a Market Overt, and yet that is, if the Owner pay the Party who bought the Horse in the Market Overt, so much as he will swear he paid *bona fide* for the Horse: But this Restitution of Horses upon the *Stat.* of 31 *Eliz.* hath no great Relation to that Restitution upon the *Stat.* of 21 *H.* 8. they being of two several Natures, therefore *Quære legem Vide postea* 18, a. *con.* and so is the constant Practice.

One challenged 36, hanged and not pressed.
2 Hawk. 461, 462.

3 *H.* 7. 12. *a.* One arraigned before *Fairfax Bryan,* and *Haugh* at *Newgate* for Felony, challenged 36, and the Question was, what should be done with him, and all the Judges of the one Bench and the other agreed, that he should be hanged and not pressed to Death, and this Rule they would have all the Judges to observe in their Circuits, notwithstanding the Opinion *tempore E.* 4. to the contrary; and yet in the very same Page it is said in another Case upon the like Challenge, the Book saith the Opinion was, that he should be pressed as a Person that refused the Law.

One abjureth for Felony. and being after taken in England he stands mute, he shall be hanged; but 26 Ass. Pl. 19 Br. Payne 12. is to the contrary, but that seemeth not to be Law.
2 Hawk. 461, 462.
As to standing mute, where the Judgement shall be to be pressed, and where proceed to Tryal, and put him upon the Jury.

30 *Ass. Pl.* 3. *Br. Payne* and *Penance* 2. One abjureth and is after taken in *England,* and demanded what he could say, why Execution should not be awarded, he stands mute, he shall be hanged, and not put to penance or pressed; because he was attainted of the Felony before by his Confession: For he cannot have the Benefit of the Sanctuary to abjure, unless he confess the Felony which is entered on Record by the Coroner; and there its said, if a Felon plead not guilty upon his Arraignment, and after stand mute before his Tryal, it is as if he had not pleaded: But if upon his Arraignment he confess the Felony, and after being demanded what he can say, why Execution should not be, he stands mute, there he shall be hanged. *Note,* It seems to me, that in the Case before, where it is said a Felon pleads not guilty, that if after, upon his Tryal he stand mute, yet the Jury shall be charged with him, and Evidence given for the King; and if he be found guilty he shall be hanged; for after the Prisoner hath pleaded once not guilty he cannot hinder the Tryal, and

and therefore I suppose that Case is to be intended when *the* Prisoner only pleaded not guilty, and being asked how he would be tryed, stands mute, and refuses the Tryal of Law, there the bare pleading of not guilty is as nothing; but in case he pleaded not guilty, and for Tryal puts himself on the Country, then if after he stands mute, yet the Court shall proceed to his Tryal, and so the Book of 15 *E.* 4. 33. *Br. p.* 9. A Felon is arraigned and pleads not guilty, and puts himself upon his Country, and then challenged 31, and thereupon is a *Tales* granted, and then he stands mute, and the Jury was charged with him and found guilty.

2 Inst. 178, 9.
2 Hawk. 464.

Vide 2 Hawk. 463. Note to Sect. 7.

In an Appeal for Felony if the Prisoner stands mute, he shall have Judgment to be pressed, as in case he had been arraigned at the King's Suit, and stands mute. 43 *Aff. pl.* 30. *Br. Payn.* 13 & 14 *E.* 4. 7. *Br. ibid.* 15.

Mute in Appeal the same Judgment as upon Indictment.

At the Sessions at the *Old Bailey* the 7*th Decemb.* 1664, one *Jone Jenes*, together with one *Thomas Wharton*, were indicted for Burglary, and she pleaded herself to be married to *Wharton*, on Purpose to be excused, being with her husband at the Burglary, and she refused to plead by the Name of *Jones*, and thereupon we called for the Jury, which found the Indictment, and in their Presence, and by their Consent *, we made the Indictment as to her Name to be *Jane Wharton alias Jones*; but we did not call her *Jane Wharton* the Wife of *Thomas Wharton*, but gave her the Addition of *Spinster*; and then she pleaded to it, and the Court told her, that if upon her Tryal, she could prove that she was married to *Wharton* before the Burglary committed, she should have the Advantage of it: But on the tryal she could not prove it, and so was found guilty, and Indictment given upon her.

Jone Jenes Wharton's Case. A Woman in the same Felony with a Man, pretends to be his Wife; the way of Indictment in that Case. 2 Hawk. 348.

At the same Sessions, at the Tryal of a Prisoner, he took Exception against the Witness against him, because he had formerly been burned in the Hand for Felony; but the Chief Justice *Hyde, Kelyng,* and *Wylde, Recorder,* being present, held that to be no Exception, and in civil Causes such Persons are frequently admitted for Witnesses; and it differs from cutting off Ears, standing in 10. One attainted of Felony and pardoned is no good Witness, *man di* so proved, disallowed.

Burning in the Hand for Felony, no Exception against his being Witness. *Bulstrode* a part 155. 2 Hawk. 609. *Modus deciman di*

＊ *Note,* the Jury Consent at the Time they are Sworn.

the

38   Murder and other Offences.

By the Statute of 18 El. 17. He who hath Clergy, is totally difcharged. Vide Membr. fol. 25.
If Clergyman burned in the Hand, and after fued Foxley's *Cafe, ter Judgment*

the Pillory or other ftigmatizing, becaufe thofe Punifhments make the Perfon Infamous, and fo he is not allowed for a Witnefs: But burning in the Hand does not fo, becaufe it cometh in the place of Purgation at the Common Law, which fuppofeth he might be not guilty, notwithftanding the Verdict. And therefore at the Common Law, he that confeffeth a Felony, could never be admitted to his Purgation, for there could be no Prefumption of not guilty againft his own Confeffion. *Vide Godbolt* 288.
to be deprived for that Caufe, prohibition. *Vide Co.* 5. *c.* 110. and it is in lieu of Purgation, which admits guilty, efpecially after Judgment and Attainder. 2 Hawk. 511, 558.

Marriot's Cafe. One committed for refufing the Oath of Allegiance, difcharged, as no fuch Oath to induce the Penalty of Premunire.

At the fame Time and Seffions, One *Ifaac Marriot*, and others were committed, and the *Mittimus* was for refufing to take the Oath of Allegiance, and fo the Juftice of the Peace thought to bring them into a Premunire; but the Court difcharged him and the Reft, becaufe the Oath intended was the Oath injoined by the Statute of 3 *Jac. Cap.* 4. and it is not an Oath of Allegiance, though it be commonly fo called; but in truth it is an Oath of Obedience, and fo the Court difcharged them, becaufe there was no fuch Oath of Allegiance, &c.

An Alien living here, is a Subject within the Statute of Quakers.

At the fame Seffions, upon the Tryal of feveral Quakers for their third Offence after two former Convictions before the Juftice of Peace upon the Statute of 16 *Car.* 2. *An Act to prevent and fupprefs feditious Conventicles;* One of them pleaded, that he was an Alien born in *France*, and fo not within the Penalty of that Act, becaufe the Statute fays, *that every Perfon above the Age of* 16 *Years, eingh a Subject of this Realm, fhall*, &c. And he faid he was no Subject, and fo not within the Law: It was agreed by us all, that if an Alien come into this Kingdom, and live under the King's Protection, that as long as he liveth here he is a Subject of this Realm, and punifhable for tranfgreffing the Laws thereof, according to *Calvin's* Cafe, *Co.* 7 *Rep.* 6, *b.* and fhall be indicted for High-Treafon, and the Indictment concludes *contra Allegianc' fuam debitam.* But if the Statute had faid been a Natural-born Subject of this Realm, then it had not extended to him, and that alfo appeareth by the penning of feveral Statutes, fome being generally Subjects, or all Subjects, &c. which extend to Aliens which live here, and other, that all Natural-born
Subjects,

Murder and other Offences. 39

Subjects, which extend to them only who are such, and not Aliens who live here, and accordingly we proceeded against him, and he had Judgment to be transported.

At the same Sessions, *Francis Trollop* was indicted for stealing the Goods of *Matthias Bowyer*, and upon the Evidence it appeared, that the Goods were not *Bowyer*'s, that he was a *Glosterhire* Carrier, and in his Journey they were stolen from him, and agreed that the Indictment was well enough, for tho' he had not the absolute Property, in the Goods, yet he had a possessory Property, for which he may maintain an Action of Trespass against any one that took them from him; and so may indict a Thief for taking his Goods, and so the Indictment is good either for stealing the Goods of the Carrier or of the right Owner.

Trollop's Case. A Carrier hath Goods delivered, and is robbed, the Indictment is good, that he stole the Goods of the Carrier.

At the same Sessions, One *Joseph Fabian*, a working Gold-smith, was indicted for falsifying Plate, and by putting in too much Copper, made it some Pieces 2*d*. in others 3*d*. 4*d*. 5*d*. 6*d*. 7*d*. in the Ounce worse than it ought to be, and then corrupted one of the Essay Masters Servants to help him to the old Marks of the *Leopard*'s Head, and other Marks which are set on Plate when it is essayed and found good, and with those Marks he marked his false Plate at his own House, and so he sold his Plate to the selling Gold-smiths, who did not mistrust it, because they saw it marked: For the Essay Master is so curious, that if the Plate be a fourth Part of a Farthing more than it ought to be, they break it in pieces, and the old Marks ought always to be broken in pieces when new Marks are made. And because the Essay Master had not caused those old Marks to be broken, he was turned out of his Office, and *Fabian*, who was found guilty, fined 100*l*. and adjudged to stand in the Pillory three Days, from Eleven of the Clock until One, that is to say, once at the *Old Change*, and another Time in *Cheapside*, and the third Time before *Goldsmiths Hall*, with a Paper in his Hat, declaring his Crime, and he was also forejudged of his Trade, that he should not use that Trade again as a Master Workman.

Fabian's Case. Goldsmith for falsifying Plate.

Judgment.

Fore-judged not to use his Trade as a Master Workman.

In

Murder and other Offences.

Hull's Case.

In the Sessions in the *Old Bailey* holden the 13 of *January* 1664, One *John Hull* was indicted for the Murder of *Henry Cambridge*, and upon the Evidence, the Case was, that there were several Workmen about building of a House by the Horse-Ferry, which House stood about 30 Foot from any High-way or common Passage, and *Hull* being a Master Workman (about Evening when the Master-workman had given over Work, and when the Labourers were putting up their Tools,) was sent by his Master to bring from the House a piece of Timber which lay two Stories high, and he went up for that piece of Timber, and before he threw it down, he cried out aloud, Stand Clear, and was heard by the Labourers, and all of them went from the Danger but only *Cambridge*, and the piece of Timber fell upon him and killed him : and my Lord Chief Justice *Hyde* held this to be Manslaughter, for he said he should have let it down by a Rope, or else at his Peril, be sure no Body is there : But my Brother *Wylde* and myself held it to be Misadventure, he doing nothing but what is usual for Workmen to do : And before he did it, crying out aloud, Stand Clear, and so gave notice if there were any near they might avoid it; and we put the Case, a Man lopping a Tree, and when the Arms of the Tree were ready to fall, calls out to them below, Take Heed, and then the Arms of the Tree fall and kill a Man, this is Misadventure; and we shewed him *Poulton de pace* 120. where the Case is put, and the Book cited, and held to be Misadventure; and we said this Case in Question is much stronger than the Case where one throws a Stone or shoots an Arrow over the Wall or House, with which one is slain, this in *Kelloway* 108 & 136. is said to be Misadventure. But we did all hold that there was a great difference betwixt the Case in Question, the House from which the Timber was thrown standing thirty Foot from the High-way or common Footpath, and the doing the same Act in the Streets of *London*; for we all agreed, that in *London*, that if one be a cleansing of a Gutter, called out to stand aside, and then throw down Rubbish, or a piece of Timber, by which a Man is killed, this is Manslaughter; being in *London*, there is a continual concourse of People passing up and down the Streets,

Manslaughter and Misadventure in what Cases.
1 Hawk. 111.
1 H.P.C. 475.
Fost. 263.
See the Rules there laid down.

London Streets and a Country-town much differ.

Streets, and a new Passenger, who did not hear him call out, and therefore the casting down any such Thing from an House into the Streets, is like the Case where a Man shoots an Arrow or Gun into a Market-place full of People, if any one be killed it is Manslaughter; because in common Presumption his Intention was to do Mischief, when he casts or shoots any Thing which may kill among a multitude of People; but in case that an House standing in a Country-town where there is no such frequency of Passengers, if a Man call out there to stand aside, and take heed, and then cast down the filth of a Gutter, &c. my Brother *Wylde* and I held that a far different Case from doing the same Thing in *London*. And because my Lord *Hyde* differed in the principal Case, it was found Specially, but I take the Law to be clear, that it is but Misadventure. Murder.
1 H.P.C. 475.
in notis.
Fost. 263.
1 H.P.C. 472.
2 Hawk. 111.
Bract. l. 3, 64.
Dalt. 1, 96.
B. Cor. 229.

At the same Sessions *James Rampton* was indicted for the Murder of his Wife; and upon the Evidence the Case was, that he being a *Hackney Coachman*, found a Soldiers Pistol in the Street, and when he came home he shewed it to his Master, and they took the Gun-stick and put it into the Pistol, and it went down into the Muffel of the Pistol, by which they thought it was not charged, and his Wife standing before him, he pulled up the Cock and the Pistol went off, and being charged with two Bullets, wounded her in the Belly, and killed her, upon which he cried out, Oh I have killed my dear Wife! and called in Neighbours, it was holden by *us all*, *that this was Manslaughter, and not only Misadventure*. *Rampton's* Case.
Manslaughter, Misadventure.
1 Hawk. 112.

Quære *.

At the Common Law, if a Man had committed several Felonies, and had been arraigned for one, and prayed his Clergy, yet he might be indicted for any other Felony, and thereupon was made the Statute of Clergy, 25 *Ed.* 3. *C.* 5. which required that a Clerk be charged with all Felonies, at once. And after that Stat. if a Man had committed several Felonies, some within Clergy and some without Clergy, and had been arraigned of one of the Felonies within Clergy and convicted of it, and his Clergy allowed for that, he was discharged thereof and could not be tried for any of the other Felonies which were committed betwixt the first Felony and the Time of the Allowance of his Clergy for it, tho' the other Felons was without Clergy allowed where may be put to answer for other Felonies notwithstanding.

Vid. Recital 8 *El. Cap.* 4.
agreed the Law so.
2 Hawk. 10.

* The learned Editor was not satisfied with this judgment. See Fost. 263, 264, 265.

Benefit

Benefit of Clergy, *Stam. pl. Cor.* 107, *b. Coke. pl. Cor.* 214. but now by the Statute of 8 *Eliz.* C. 4. if Clergy be allowed, that both discharge all other Felonies within Clergy; but he may be arraigned for a Felony, for which Clergy is not allowable, though it were committed before his Clergy were allowed: *Co. Pl. Cor.* 214. But now by the Statute of 18 *Eliz.* C. 7. it seems that although Clergy hath been allowed for one Felony he may be indicted for another Felony also within Clergy committed before the Time that his Clergy was allowed; for that Statute of 18 *Eliz.* speaks generally that all Persons admitted to the Benefit of the Clergy shall notwithstanding answer to all other Felonies whereof they shall be indicted or appealed, and not being thereof before acquitted, convicted, attainted, or pardoned; and if this be not the meaning of this Statute, then it is to no purpose; for all the other Cases where Clergy was not allowable were helped by the Statute of 8 *Eliz. Cap.* 4. before mentioned. And my Lord Chief Justice *Hyde* told me that when his Uncle Sir *Nicholas Hyde* was Chief Justice, he meeting with a notorious Rogue for stealing of Sheep and Cows all being within Clergy, caused him to be tryed upon one of the Indictments, and presently called the Ordinary, and upon his return, that he read, he allowed him his Clergy; and then after he tryed him at the same Assizes upon the other Indictments, upon which he was convicted, and demanded his Clergy, which he denied him, because he had had his Clergy once allowed him, and so the Fellow was hanged: But yet the Practice at the Sessions at the *Old Bailey* is contrary to this, and so that Statute of 18 *Eliz.* made of no Effect. *But notwithstanding the Practice is conceived to be according to Law.*

Le Mott's Case. Burglary *in fraudem Legis.*
1 Hawk. 161.
1 H.P.C. 507.
1 H.P.C 552.
4 Black.Com. 225.

At the Sessions I inquired of *Le Mott*'s Case, which was adjudged in the Time of the late Troubles, and my Brother *Wylde* told me, that the Case was this: That Thieves came with intent to rob him, and finding the Door locked up, pretending they came to speak with him, and thereupon a Maid Servant opened the Door, and they came in and robbed him, and this being in the Night Time, this was adjudged Burglary, and the Persons hanged; for their Intention being to rob, and getting the Door open by a false Pretence this was *in fraudem Legis,*

Murder and other Offences. 43

gis, and so they were guilty of Burglary, though they did not actually break the House, for this was in Law, an actual breaking, being obtained by fraud to have the Door opened; as if men pretend a Warrant to a Constable, and bring him along with them, and under that Pretence rob the House, if it be in the Night, this is Burglary.

At the Goal delivery in the *Old Bailey*, 5 *April*, 1665, Lord Chief Justice *Hyde*, myself, and my Brother *Wylde*, Recorder of *London*, then present, one *Richard Farre*, and *Eleanor Chadwick* were indicted for breaking the House of *Robert Stanyer*, and putting his Wife in fear, and stealing from thence several Goods; and upon the Evidence, the Case was that Mrs. *Stanyer* whose House was robbed, had for many Years lived from her Husband, and hired this House, and a Lease was drawn up for the House in her Husband's Name, which he refused to seal, and said he would have nothing to do with, but the Landlord and she agreed, and she constantly paid the Rent, and had the House very well furnished, and had Plate, Jewels, and Houshold Stuff of very good Value, and *Farre* the Prisoner, and *Eleanor Chadwick*, who lived with him as his Whore, and so had done a great while, intending to rifle her House, laid this Design, viz. *Farre* went to an Attorney of the *Common Pleas*, and told him that Mrs. *Stanyer* was his Tenant and in Arrear for Rent, and he had no way to get her out but by *ejection. firmæ*, and thereupon, he according to the Way now used, made a casual Ejector of his own and delivered a Declaration, and *Eleanor Chadwick* made false Oath in the Common Pleas, that she had delivered a Copy of that Declaration to the Tenant in Possession, and thereupon Judgment was obtained (according to the Course) against the casual Ejector, and a Writ to the Sheriff to deliver Possession, and thereupon *Farre* got the Sheriff's Bailiffs to execute the Writ, and turn Mrs. *Stanyer* out of Possession, and at the same time *Farre* took out a *Latitat* against Mrs. *Stanyer*, supposing a debt, and at the same Time arrested her and would take no Bail, but caused her to be carried to *Newgate*, and then *Farre* and *Chadwick* went to rifle her Goods in the House, and broke open Cubbards and

Farr's and *Chadwick's* Case.
1 Hawk. 16;.
1 H.P.C. 552.
Foster 77.
Robbers *in fraudem Legis* by colour of Lawful Pretences.

Vide *postea* and *Coffee's* Case.
1 Hawk. 136.
1 Sid. 254, S.C.
Raym. 276.

G 2   Trunks,

Murder and other Offences.

Trunks, and took away Jewels and Plate, and carried them into his own House, and hid them there, and carried away divers of the Goods by Night, and took the Pewter which had her Husband's Arms upon it, and got them taken out, and sold other of the Goods; and after upon Complaint to my Lord Chief Justice, by his Warrant *Farre's* House was searched, and the Jewels and Plate there found, and divers other Goods; and *Farre* and *Chadwick*, upon Examination by my Lord Chief Justice, were sent by him to *Newgate*, and now this Indictment preferred against them, and *Farre* being asked what colour of Title he had to the House, could pretend none, but it appeared that the true Landlord had received the Rent of it for many Years, and that no Rent at all was behind. And *Farre* being asked what cause of Action he had against Mrs. *Stanyer* to cause her to be arrested, could pretend none; and being likewise asked what colour he had to break open Trunks and Cubbards, and to take the Goods and sell them, and cause the Coat of Arms to be expunged, he could make no pretence; and it was agreed by us all, that although they had made use of the Law and Officers of Law to get the Possession and to arrest the Woman, yet if all this done in *fraudem Legis* with intent to Rob, this course was so far from excusing the Robbery, that it heightened the Offence by abusing the Law, and the Process of it without Colour of Title, &c. As *Co. Pl. Cor.* 64. if Thieves pretending to be robbed, raise Hue and Cry, and call a Constable in the Night, and cause him to search an House on pretence the Thieves are there, and thereupon, by Command of the Constable, the Door is opened, and they go in, and then rob the House, this is Burglary, though the House was not actually broke open by them, but opened at the Command of the Constable, for this being in *fraudem Legis* shall be accounted as an actual breaking in them, and so was *Le Mott*'s Case adjudged, which is in this Book the next Case before this, and so it hath been adjudged, that if Goods are distrained, and put in a Pound, and one who hath a Design to steal them, goeth to the Sheriff and gets a Replevin for these Goods, and by colour of this Replevin, the Goods are delivered to him, and he driveth them away and sells them, having no colour of Title to them, this is Felony. And we also agreed, that altho' Mr. *Stanyer* the Husband did not dwell

in

in this House, and refused to have to do with it, yet the Indictment was well, for breaking open his Dwelling House, for whatever the Wife hath is the Husband's in Law, and it cannot be said to be the Wive's House, and so Direction was given to the Jury, that if they did believe that the Prisoners had done all this with an intent to rob, they ought to find them guilty, and the Jury did find them guilty, and both of them had Judgment to be hanged, and were executed accordingly.

At the same Sessions, one *Edward Parret* was in the Place where the Prisoners use to stand at the Goal-delivery, who was in for Murder, for which he had afterwards Judgment, and while he was there, one *John Copeland* a *Scotchman*, being in very good Clothes, went in thither under colour to see him, and watching the Time when the Keepers were busie, he opened the little Door which was bolted, and went out, and *Parret* the Prisoner followed him, and the Keeper of the outward Door not knowing them, opened that to them, and they both went together out of the Yard, and run down By-Allies into *Shew-Lane*, and so to *White-Fryers*, but the Keepers presently missing the Prisoner, made after them, and being told which Way they run, overtook them in *White-Fryers*, and brought them both back, and thereupon *Copeland* was indicted for Felony, for rescuing *Parret*, being indicted for Murder, and upon the Evidence it was sworn that after they were taken, *Copeland* said he had done nothing but what he ought to help away his Friend, who was in danger of his Life, and on this Evidence he was found guilty, and on his Request he being to have Clergy, it was allowed to be put into the King's Pardon, amongst those Prisoners of that Nature, who were to be sent beyond the Sea, it having been lately used, that for Felonies within Clergy, if the Prisoner desire it, not to give his Book, but to procure a conditional Pardon from the King, and send them beyond the Sea to serve 5 Years in some of the King's Plantations, and then to have Land there assigned them according to the use in those Plantations, for Servants after the Time expired, with a Condition in the Pardon to be void if they do not go, or if they return into *England* during seven Years, or after without the King's Licence *.

Copeland's Case. Rescuing a Felon by secret helping him away from the Place where Prisoners are put at the Time of Tryals in the Old Bailey. Vide Stamford *Pl. Cor.* 30, 31, 32. Of breaking Prison and Rescous.

* As to Transportation, see 1 Hawk. 244, Ap. 13th, and 2 Hawk. 514, Chap. 35, continued per totum.

House robbed in the Night after Goods brought into it, and whilst he is removing thither.
1 Hawk. 162.
1 H.P.C. 556.
in notis.

At the same Sessions one was indicted for Burglary, for breaking open a House in the Night, and stealing away Goods, and upon the Evidence, the Case was, that he whose Goods were stolen, had hired the House which was broke open in the Night, and had the Possession delivered him, and had removed several of his Goods from the House he formerly lived in, to the House which he had newly hired, but lay in his first House till he had removed the Rest of his Goods, and fitted his new House, by setting up Beds to lie there: And in this Time, before he had lodged in his new House, that House was broke open in the Night, and his Goods stolen. And it was doubted whether this were Burglary, because some of us held it could not be said to be his Mansion-house before such Time as he had ever inhabited it, but others of us said it would be a very mischievous Case that Thieves might take such an Opportunity to rob in the Night, and have Benefit of the Clergy; and if a Man have a Dwelling-house, and on Occasion, he and his Family be out of it all Night, and then it is robbed, this is without Question Burglary, and in this Case by taking the House to inhabit, and bringing his Goods thither in order to inhabit, and forbearing the Lodging only untill his Goods and Beds can be set up, this might well be called his Mansion-house, and should be so esteemed in Law, *Ideo Quære Legem.*

Gardner's Case. Soldiers breaking open Houses by Warrant to search, &c. Tremaine 355.

At the same Sessions Mr. *Martin Gardner*, and other Officers and their Soldiers, to the number of Nineteen, were indicted for breaking open the House of *Jonathan Hutchison* near *Cheapside* in the Day time, and putting him in fear, &c. and stealing away several Goods, and upon the Evidence, the Case was that the Lord *Arlington*, the King's Secretary, by Order from the King made a Warrant to apprehend certain Persons named in the Warrant being dangerous Persons; and this Warrant was directed to one of the King's Messengers, and he having Notice that those Persons named in the Warrant were at a meeting in *Hutchison's* House, desired those Soldiers to assist him in the taking of them, whereupon they came to the House, and broke open the Door, and apprehended some of them, but in the doing of it, some of the common Soldiers without the Knowledge of their Officers, and against

against their command took away a Cloak, and some small Things out of the House, but the Witnesses could not tell which of the Soldiers they were, but said, my Lord *Mayor* who took the Examinations could fit them upon the Persons; and my Lord *Mayor* being now absent, upon Occasion of the Death of Sir *Thomas Vyner*, who died this Morning, I conceiving it necessary to say something to satisfy the Citizens and others standing by, did to this Effect declare the Law, That if several Persons come into a House together with an intent to steal, if but one of them steal Goods, they are all equally guilty. 2. That this Warrant now produced was not sufficient to justify the breaking open the Doors of the House, and Soldiers ought not on any Pretence to break open Houses unless they have with them a Civil Officer, as Justice of the Peace, or Constable. 3. That if Persons have a Warrant to apprehend any one, and they in order to execute the Warrant break open a Door, and mistake the Law in that Point; this breaking of the Door maketh them Trespassers, but can never be interpreted to make them guilty of Felony; for their Design was not to commit Felony, and there must be always a felonious Intent to make a Felony. 4. If after a Door broken with intent to apprehend a Person, any of the Company take away any of the Goods from the House, this is Felony in the Person that did it, and in none of the Rest; unless it can be proved that any of the Rest were assenting to the taking of the Goods, and then it is Felony in as many as consented; and after this done, by reason the Evidence could not be made out without the Examinations taken by my Lord *Mayor* and he was absent, therefore I discharged the Jury of them, and ordered Bail to be taken of them to appear the next Goal-delivery *.

Where the breaking open a House Felony, and where not. 2 Hawk. 441.

By Colour of a Warrant. 2 Hawk. 442.

Ante 26, and Post 52. 2 H.P.C. 295. Sed Vide Post. 16, 39, 75, 328.

Vide, This Book before, concerning Restitution of stolen Goods to the Prosecutor. If upon his Evidence, or Evidence proved by him, the Thief be convicted, I have made a great inquiry, and find that my Brother *Wylde* was in the Right, for the Words of the *Stat.* of 21 *H.* 8. *C.* 11. are general, that where the Thief is convicted at the Prosecution of the Party robbed, there the Party robbed shall have Restitution, and taketh no Notice whether

Ante 35.

* Discharging the Jury of Offenders, seems all through this Book, to have been the Practice in the Time of Kelyng: see the Cases in the Margin, but see the contrary are the Rules then referred to.

the

the Goods be fold in a Market Overt, or not; fo by that Statute the Common Law is altered as to that Point. And for that *Stat.* of 31 *Eliz. Cap.* 12. concerning Horfes ftolen, and fold in a Market Overt, the Owner may have them again if he make claim within fix Months, and pay the Buyer what he paid *bona fide*, that is nothing to this Cafe. For that Statute giveth that kind of Reftitution as to Horfes, altho' there be no Profecution. And for the Bifhop of *Worcefter*'s Cafe, 'tis true, the Inference of the Book is as it is there faid; but the main Point was not there in Queftion, altho' in thofe Times there was a doubtful Opinion what the Law was; and I fpake with Mr. *Lee* a very good Clerk, who hath attended the Seffions at the *Old Bailey* above forty Years; and I afked him how the Practice there was, and he told me it was doubted till about 4 & 5 *Car.* 1. And then Juftice *Jones*, and feveral other Judges advifed about it, and did refolve that the Party who loft the Goods and profecuted the Felon to Conviction fhould have Reftitution of his Goods which were ftolen, notwithftanding they were fold in a Market Overt, and ever fince that Time he fays the Practice hath been accordingly. And if any one plead to a Writ of Reftitution in fuch a Cafe, that he bought the Goods in a Market Overt; ever fince the Refolution the other Party prefently demurred unto it, and had Judgment: And I think it to be a very good Refolution warranted by the Words of the *Stat.* of 21 *H.* 8. and tends to the advancement of Juftice to make Men profecute Felons, and it will difcourage Perfons from buying ftolen Goods, tho' in a Market Overt; for under that pretence Men buy Goods there for a fmall Value of Perfons whom they have reafon to fufpect, which Practice this Refolution will abate.

Moore 360.

Vide Co. fur Magna Charta; p. 714. accord. notwithftanding a Sale in a Market Overt, in Cafe of an Appeal at Common Law; And *Stat.* 21 *H.*8. faith that Reftitution fhall be made in cafe the Thief be convicted at the Profecution of him who loft the Goods, as in the Cafe of an Appeal at Common Law.

Coke's Magna Charta is exprefs in Point, that upon the *Stat.* of 21 *H.* 8. the Owner who Profecutes fhall have Reftitution, notwithftanding a Sale in Market Overt. *Note*, If Goods be ftolen, and not waived in flight, nor feized by fome of the King's Officers, as fufpected to be ftolen, there the Party that is robbed may take his Goods again, or bring an Action for them, altho' he doth not Profecute.

Profecute. *Vide Co. 5. Rep. Foxley's Cafe* 109. *Stamford Pl. Caron.* 186. *b.* But if the Goods be waived by the Felon in his Flight or in Cafe they be not waived, yet if they be feized by any of the King's Officers as fufpecting them to be ftolen, there the Party fhall not have Reftitution, unlefs the Thief be convicted at his Profecution, *Vide Stamford, Pl. Cor.* 186. *b.* And in fuch Cafes the Party fhall have Reftitution only for fuch Goods as are expreffed in the indictment, and not for any other Goods tho' ftolen at the fame time, if they are omitted out of the indictment, becaufe by that omiffion the Chief might have efcaped, *Co. 5. Rep. Foxley's Cafe* 110. *Vide* for thefe matters *Stamford, Pl. Cor. Title Frefh Sute,* 165. and *Title Wayfe,* 185. and the *fame Book Title* *. 2 Hawk. 248, 249, 250, 251, 252, 467, 468.

The Queftion, whether at this day there needs two Witneffes to convict a man of High Treafon, hath grown only upon the Opinion of *Co. Pl. Cor.* 25, 26. where amongft other things, he delivers an Opinion that at the Common Law, two Witneffes are needful in Cafes of Treafon, and cites many Books in the Margin; but none of them warrant any fuch Opinion; and there are many things in his Pofthumous Works, efpecially in his Pleas of the Crown concerning Treafons, and in his Jurifdiction of the Courts concerning Parliaments, which lie under a Sufpicion, whether they received no Alteration, they coming out in the time of that which is called the *Long Parliament,* in the time of that defperate Rebellion againft *King Charles* the firft. But certain it is, there are many Errours in thofe places; but as to the main Queftion, it feemeth to me very plain by the exprefs Words of the *Stat.* of 1 *E.* 6. c. 12. that at the Common Law one Witnefs was fufficient in High Treafon. For the Words of the *Stat.* are, no Perfon after the firft day of *February, then next coming, fhould be indicted, convicted, &c. for any Offence of Treafon, &c. Unlefs fuch Offender be aceufed by Two fufficient Witneffes,* which proveth ftrongly, as I think, that before that time one Witnefs was enough, and, in all Cafes at Common Law, Proof by one Witnefs is fufficient, and no authority, that I can find, in any Book is otherwife, fo that I take the neceffity of two Witneffes was induced by the *Stat.* in 1 *E.* 6. and then the Force of that Statute is taken away by the 1 *&* 2 *Ph, & Ma. cap.* 10. which altho'

One Witnefs is enough in Treafon, as it feemeth to me. 2 H P.C. 287. 2 Hawk. 602, 3 contra.

H

*Title Appeals. St. Pl. Cor. 66, as I believe.

altho' it were in the general a Law which expired with that Queen, being made for preservation of her Person, yet that Clause in that Statute, that Trials for Treasons shall be according to the course of Common Law, is a perpetual Clause, and restoreth the Common Law as it was before the *Stat.* 1 of *E.* 6. and the *Stat.* 1 & 2 *Phil.* & *Ma. cap.* 11. which is the next Chapter concerning Treasons, in counterfeiting Monies, saith, that the Offenders shall be indicted, convicted, and attainted by such like Evidence, and in such manner as they might have been before the first Year of the late K. *E.* 6. which points expresly to the time when two Witnesses were required, and which by this Statute appeared not to be at the Common Law *.

Vid. Stat. 1. *Jac. c.* 21.
Sale to Brokers not alter the Property.

That *Brokers*, as they are now used for taking to pawn or buying of Apparel, Bedding, Plate, Jewels, &c. is an unlawful Trade, and enacted, that no Sale to such Persons in *London*, *Westminster*, *Southwark*, or within two miles thereof, alters any property; and that if they refuse to shew any such Goods so pawned or sold, they forfeit the double value: and so there is a difference betwixt the ancient *Brokers* and these new *Brokers*, so that by the Statute if any stolen Goods be bought by them, the party may have his Action against them for the Goods, whether he prosecute the Felon or not, for the property remains to the Owner, notwithstanding such sale.

Hood's Case. Jurors fined for finding Manslaughter contrary to direction of the Court, See before. This course of fining was used in those Days, but since condemned, and never since used barely for giving a Verdict contrary to Evidence.

Memorandum, at *Lent* Circuit at *Winchester,* 18 *Car.* 2. One *Henry Hood* was indicted for the Murder of *John Newen,* and upon the Evidence it appeared, that he killed him without any provocation, and thereupon I directed the Jury, that it was Murder; for the Law in that Case intended malice; and I told them they were judges of the matter of fact, viz. whether *Newen* died by the hand of *Hood*; but whether it was Murder or Manslaughter, that was matter in Law, in which they were to observe the direction of the Court. But notwithstanding they would find it only Manslaughter; whereupon I took the Verdict, and fined the Jury, of which *John Goldwier* was the Foreman, 5*l.* a piece, and committed them to Goal till they found Sureties to appear

* But this Doubt is removed by Statute 7. W. 3 C. 3. Vide Foster 1 Disc. on H. T. Cap. 3. p 221. 2 Ed.
† But coli to Pawnbrokers in Great Britain. Vide 30 Geo. 2. c. 24, and 24 Geo. 3. c. 42.

Murder and other Offences.

appear at the next Assizes, and in the mean time to be of the good Behaviour: but after, upon the Petition of the Jurors, I took down their fines to 40s. a piece, which they all paid, and entered in Recognizance, &c. *

At the same Assizes at *Winchester*, the Clerk appointed by the Bishop to give Clergy to the Prisoners, being to give it to an old Thief; I directed him to deal clearly with me, and not to say *legit* in case he could not read; and thereupon he delivered the Book to him, and I perceived the Prisoner never looked upon the Book at all, and yet the Bishop's Clerk, upon the demand of *legit* or *non legit*, answered *legit*; and thereupon I wished him to consider, and told him I doubted he was mistaken, and bid the Clerk of the Assizes ask him again, *legit* or *non legit*, and he answered again something angrily, *legit*: Then I bid the Clerk of the Assizes not to record it, and I told the Parson he was not the Judge whether he read or not, but a Ministerial Officer to make a true Report to the Court. And so I caused the Prisoner to be brought near, and delivered him the Book, and then the Prisoner confessed he could not read; whereupon I told the Parson he had reproached his Function, and unpreached more that day than he could preach up again in many days; and because it was his personal Offence and Misdemeanor, I fined him 5 *Marks*, and did not fine the Bishop, as in case he had failed to provide an Ordinary.

My Brother *Archer*, upon discourse, told me he well remembered the Case of *Mr. Ford, a Gent.* in *Grays Inn*, who in the time when *Sir Nich. Hyde* was Chief Justice, was indicted of Murder in the King's Bench, and upon the Evidence, the case was that *Mr. Ford* with other Company, was in the *Vine Tavern* in *Holborn*, in a Room, and some other Company, bringing with them some Women of ill Fame, would needs have the Room where *Mr. Ford* was, and turn him out, to which *Mr. Ford* answered, that if they had civilly desired it, they might have had it, but he would not be turned out by force, and thereupon they drew their Swords on *Mr. Ford*, and his Company, and *Mr. Ford*, drew his Sword, killed one of them, and it was adjudged justifiable.

Side notes: The Ordinary fined, for saying the Prisoner did read when he could not, for endeavouring to abuse the Court. 2 Hawk. 506.

Ante 28.
2 H. P. C.

2 Hawk. 506, 7.

Mr. Ford's Case.
Killing a Man in defence of his own Possession of a Room in a Tavern justifiable.
1 Hawk. 110.
1 Hawk. 125.
Prin. P. L. 225.
Vide Mawgridge's Case.
Post 119.
Holt 484.
9 St. Tr. 61.
Memorand.
To inquire of this Case †.

H 2

* But see Bushel's Case. Vaughan 135. and 2 Hawk. 225.
† This Case continues to be doubted, whether it be Law. Vide Foster in notis 274.

Murder and other Offences.

Jones' and *Bever's* Case.
1 Hawk. 163.
2 Hawk. 500.
Ante 27.

At the Goal-delivery in the *Old Bailey*, 19 *February* 1665, *John Jones* and *Philip Bever*, were indicted for Burglary for breaking the King's House at *Whitehal*, and stealing from thence the Goods of the Lord Cornbury, and were found not Guilty; and after were indicted for the same Burglary, and stealing the Goods of Mr. *Nunnesy*: and we agreed that they being once acquitted for the Burglary, could not be indicted again for the same Burglary, but might be indicted for stealing the Goods of Mr. *Nunnesy* according as it was formerly resolved in *Turner's* Case. Vide ante*. But in this case when we saw the Evidence not sufficient to prove the stealing of my Lord *Cornbury*'s Goods, we might have discharged the Jury and so taken no Verdict; and then he might have been indicted for that Burglary, and stealing the Goods of Mr. *Nunnesy*.

2 Hawk. 527.
2 H.P.C. 295.
Ante 26, and 47.
And References ibid.

Post. contra, 30.

Burglary, Country House and City House.
1 Hawk. 162.

Memorandum, Mr. *Lee*, the Clerk of the Peace for *London*, then told me, that about twenty Years since in the Case of Mr. *Gardiner*, who was a Citizen, and had a House in the City where he usually lived in the Winter, and another House in the Country where he usually lived in Summer; and while he and his Family were in the Country, his house in the City was broken open in the Night, and his Goods stolen; no Person being in the House, and it was adjudged Burglary, for it was his Mansion House.

Post. 68.

Memorandum, That my Brother *Twisden* shewed me a Report which he had of a Charge given by Justice *Jones* to the Grand Jury at the King's-Bench-Barr in *Michaelmas Term*, 9 *Car*. 1. In which he said, that Poisoning another was Murder at Common Law. And the Statute of 1 *E*. 6†. was but declaratory of the Common Law, and an Affirmation of it. He cited *Vaux* and *Ridley*'s Case. If one drinks Poison by the Provocation or Persuasion of another, and dieth of it, this is Murder in the Person that persuaded it. And he took

2 Hawk. 52, 53.
Principals in Murder, tho' absent.
Post. 349.

this difference: if *A*. give Poison to *J. S.* to give to *J. D.* and *J. S.* knowing it to be Poison, give it to *J. D.* who taketh it in the absence of *J. S.* and dieth of it. In this Case *J. S.* who gave it to *J. D.* is Principal. And *A.* who gave the Poison to *J. S.* and was absent when it was taken, is but accessary before the Fact: But

---

* Page 30.
† See an Account of the Reasons of this Act. Post. 68, 69, 70, 71.

But if *A.* buyeth Poison for *J. S.* and *J. S.* in the absence of *A.* taketh it, and dieth of it; in this case *A.* though he be absent, yet he is Principal: so it is if *A.* giveth Poison to *B.* to give unto *C.* and *B.* not knowing it to be Poison, but believing it to be a good Medicine, giveth it to *C.* who dieth of it; in this case *A.* who is absent is Principal, or else a Man should be murdered and there should be no Principal: for *B.* who knew nothing of the Poison, is in no fault, tho' he gave it to *C.* So if *A.* puts a Sword into the hand of a Mad Man, and bids him kill *B.* with it, and then *A.* goeth away, and the Mad Man kills *B.* with the Sword as *A.* commanded him, this is Murder in *A.* tho' absent, and he is Principal: for it is no Crime in the Mad Man who did the Fact, by reason of his Madness, and he said that this Case was lately before himself and Baron *Trevor* at the Assizes at *Hereford*. A Woman after she had two Daughters by her Husband Eloped from him and lived with another Man. And afterwards one of her Daughters came to her, and she asked her how doth your Father, to which her Daughter answered, that he had a Cold, to which his Wife replied, here is a good Powder for him, give it to him in his Posset; and on this the Daughter carried home the Powder, and told all this that her Mother had said to her, and to her other Sister, who in her absence gave the Powder to her Father in his Posset, of which he died. And he said, that upon Conference with all the Judges, it was resolved that the Wife was Principal in the Murder, and also the Man with whom she run away, he being proved to be advising in the Poison; but the two Daughters were in no Fault, they both being ignorant of the Poison, and accordingly the Man was Hang'd, and the Mother Burnt.

2 Hawk. 443. Person absent Principal in Murder, where the Person who did the Fact is not guilty, because of Madness. 1 Hawk. 3. Dalt. 533. 1 H.P.C. 617.

Persons absent Principal in Murder. 2 Hawk. 443. Post 349.

Memorandum, that upon Saturday the 28 of *April* 1666 *An.* 18 *Car.* 2. All the Judges of *England*, viz. Myself, *J. K.* Lord Chief Justice of the King's Bench; Sir *Or. Bridgeman*, Lord Chief Justice of the Common Pleas, Sir *Matthew Hales*, Chief Baron of the Exchequer, my Brother *Atkins*, Brother *Twisden*, Brother *Tyrell*, Brother *Turner*, Brother *Browne*, Brother *Windham*, Brother *Archer*, Brother *Raynsford*, and Brother *Morton*, met together at *Serjeant's Inn* in *Fleet-street*, to consider of *S. C.*

Resolution of all the Judges, on Occasion of the Trial of Lord *Morely*. 2 Hawk. 598. 1 Lev. 180. 1 Sid. 277. 1 Keb. 896. 2 Keb. 19. 7 St. Tr. 421.

of such things as might in point of Law, fall out in the Trial of the Lord *Morly*, who was on Monday to be tryed by his Peers for a Murder, and we did all *una voce* resolve several things following, *part* 1. First it was agreed that upon the Letter of the Lord High Steward directed to us, we were to attend at the Tryal in our Scarlet Robes, and the Chief Judges in their Collars of SS. which I did accordingly; but my Lord *Bridgman* was absent, being suddenly taken with the Gout, the Chief Baron had not his Collar of SS. having left it behind him in the Country; but we all were in Scarlet, but no body then had a Collar of SS. but myself, for the Reasons aforesaid.

Vide Moor's Rep. 621. resolved by all the Judges, that on a Tryal by Peers the Prisoner can not challenge any of the Peers that are returned on his Jury. Habit of the Judges at the Tryal.

2. It was resolved, that in case the Peers who are Tryers after the Evidence given, and the Prisoner withdrawn, and they gone to consult of their Verdict, should desire to speak with any of the Judges to have their Opinion upon any point of Law, that if the Lord Steward spoke to us to go, we should go to them; but when the Lords asked us any Question, we should not deliver any Opinion, but let them know we were not to deliver any private Opinion without conference with the rest of the Judges, and that to be done openly in Court: and this, notwithstanding the President in the Case of the Earl of *Castlehaven**, was thought prudent in regard of ourselves, as well as for the avoiding Suspicion, which might grow by private Opinions, all Resolutions of Judges being always done in Publick.

If Advice asked in private of the Judges by the Peers.

3. Although we were not all agreed in the President of the Lord *Dacre*'s Case, cited by *Sir E. Coke* in the Pleas of the Crown, *p.* 29, & 30. that the Judges may deliver any Opinion in open Court, in the absence of the Prisoner; yet it was agreed, that if the Lord Steward should, in open Court, demand any of our Opinions in any thing, tho' in the absence of the Prisoner, we were to give an Answer to the Question the Lord High Steward should demand of us, we being call'd to assist the Court, and the demand of any Question in such case being referred to the Discretion of the High Steward.

If asked in Court by the High Steward in absence of Prisoner.

4. It

---

* I cannot after my best research find this Case.

4. It was resolved by us all, that in case any of the Witnesses which were examined before the Coroner, were dead or unable to Travel, and Oath made thereof, that then the examinations of such Witnesses, so dead or unable to Travel might be read, the Coroner first making Oath that such Examinations are the same which he took upon Oath, without any Addition or Alteration whatsoever.

Witnesses examined by the Coroner, dead or not able to Travel. 2 Hawk. 605. Sum. 262, 263.

5. That in case Oath should be made that any Witness who had been examined by the Coroner, and was then absent, was detained by the means or procurement of the Prisoner, and the Opinion of the Judges asked whether such Examination might be read, we should answer, that if their Lordships were satisfied by the Evidence they had heard, that the Witness was detained by means or procurement of the Prisoner, then the Examination might be read, but whether he was detained by the Means or Procurement of the Prisoner, was matter of Fact, of which we were not Judges, but their Lordships.

Witnesses detained by procurement of Prisoner. 2 Hawk. 605. 2 Keb. 19.

6. Agreed, that if a Witness who was examined by the Coroner be absent, and Oath is made that they have used all their Endeavours to find him and cannot find him, that is not sufficient to authorize the reading of such Examination.

Witness fought for and not found. 2 Hawk. 605.

7. Agreed, that no words, be they what they will, are in Law such a Provocation, as if a Man kill another for words only will diminish the Offence of killing a Man from Murder to be Manslaughter: as suppose one call another son of a Whore, or give him the Lie, and thereupon he to whom the words are given, kill the other, this is Murder. But if upon ill words, both the Parties suddainly Fight, and one kill the other, this is but Manslaughter, for it is a combat betwixt two upon a suddain heat, which is the legal description of Manslaughter; and we were all of Opinion that the Statute of 1 *Jac.* for Stabbing a Man not having first struck, nor having any Weapon drawn, was only a Declaration of the Common Law, and made to prevent the inconveniencies of Juries, who were apt to believe that to be a Provocation to extenuate a Murder, which in Law was not.

a Dagger kill the other. 1 Hawk. 116. Fost. 298.

Words only, no Provocation to lessen the Offence of killing a Man from Murder to be Manslaughter. 1 Hawk. 123. 1 Hawk. 124. 1 H.P.C. 456. Fost. 290. Vide Crompton's Just. 23. a, b. Two to play at Tables and fall out suddainly, and one with

Agreed,

If there be a Quarrel, and a reasonable Time before they Fight, it is Murder.
1 Hawk. 122, 123.
V. Crompt. Just. 23. Two fall out suddainly and Fight presently, and one kill the other it is but Manslaughter;

8. Agreed, that if upon words two Men grow to Anger, and afterwards they suppress that Anger, and then fall into other Discourses, or have other Diversions for such a space of time as in reasonable intendment, their heat might be cooled, and some time after they draw one upon another, and Fight, and one is killed, this is Murder, because being attended with such Circumstances as it is reasonably supposed to be a deliberate Act, and a premeditated Revenge upon the first Quarrel; but the Circumstances of such an Act being matter of Fact, the Jury are Judges of those Circumstances.

so if after they have quarrelled, they presently go into the Field and Fight, and one kills the other, 'tis but Manslaughter; For all is one continued Act of Fury But if two fall out suddainly, and before any blows presently appoint to go to the Field and Fight, and one kill the other, this is Murder, because it appeareth by choosing a fit place to fight, their Reason was above their Passion, and so a deliberate Act. *Vide Crompt. Just. p. 25.* acordant.

This following Report I took out of Justice Spelman's *Original Reports, which I had from* Sir Jeffry Palmer *Attorney General, which Report is cited,* Co. Pl. Cor. 29 & 30.

11 St. Tr. 10.
2 Hawk. 6.

* A Peer cannot waive his Tryal by Peers.
2 Hawk. 597.

The Lord *Dacres*'s Case, who was indicted for Treason before Commissioners of *Oyer* and *Terminer* in the County of *Cumberland*, for adhering to the Scots, the King's Enemies, and tried by his Peers 26 H. 8.* *Thomas* Duke of *Norfolk* being High Steward; and the day before all the Judges assembled to resolve certain Questions which might arise upon the said Tryal, so that if any Question should be asked them they might resolve *una voce*, and one Question was, whether the Prisoner might waive his Tryal by his Peers, and be tryed by the Country, and they all agreed he could not. For the Statute of *Magna Charta* is in the Negative, *Nec super eum ibimus nisi per legale judicium parium suorum*, this is at the King's Suit upon an indictment.

Verdict of the greatest number, good if twelve.
Foss. 247.

2. It was agreed by most of the Judges, that if all the Peers do not agree in their Verdict, then the Verdict of the greatest part of them is a good Verdict, so that there be Twelve or more; (therefore the use is never to have less than twenty three Peers for *Tryers*, because that is the least number to be sure of twelve to be of one Mind) And after the Prisoner was arraigned, and askt whether

he

Murder and other Offences.

he was Guilty or not Guilty: he desired respit to consider, because the indictment was long, and contained many things; but the High Steward told him, he must plead to the Treason, or else Judgment would be given against him as a Traitor, and thereupon he pleaded not Guilty. When he was asked how he would be tryed, and he took long time to consider, and would not have put himself upon his Peers; but at last the High Steward told him that he must give Judgment against him as a Traitor, unless he put himself upon his Peers, as against one who refused the Tryal of Law; and thereupon he put himself for his Tryal upon his Peers; and after Evidence was given, and the Prisoner withdrawn from the Bar, and the Lords gone to consider of their Verdict, they sent to the Lord Steward to speak with him; and he thereupon desired the advice of the Judges; and they advised him that he could not do so unless the Prisoner was present at the Bar. And afterwards the Peers desired the Lord Steward that one *Christopher Dacres*, Uncle to the Lord *Dacres*, who was in the *Tower* for the same Treason, might be sent for to be examined, if the L. *Dacres* did command him to go to the Lord *Maxie* to treat with him in favour of the *Scots*: and the Lord *Steward*, by the advice of the Judges, told them, that could not be done, all the Evidence being given already, and also he was not a necessary Witness, being Uncle to the Prisoner, and not supposed that he would give Evidence against him, so after, in the absence of the Prisoner (as the Course is) the Lords gave the Verdict, and found him not Guilty, and then the Prisoner was brought to the Bar, and the Lord *Steward* did rehearse the Verdict, and gave Judgment that he should be discharged paying his Fees.

And amongst the Judges, a Question was moved whether the Court might be adjourned to the next day, and they agreed it might, but it hath not been done.

Another Question was moved among them, that if the Peers did not agree, so that the Court was adjourned till the next day, what should be done with the Peers who were the Tryers? And some Judges held they were to be kept together all night, but others held, because they were not sworn, for the great Trust reposed in them, and presumed to be in them, they might go to their own Houses every one by himself.

(57)

2 Hawk. 464.
Sum. 226.
2 H. P. C 317.
Skinner 145.
Savile 56.
Dyer 205.
1 Inst. 177.
Co. Lit. 391.
3 Inst. 14, 30.
S. P. C. 150.
2 Hawk. 597.

The High Steward not to speak to the Peers in the Absence of the Prisoner.

2 Hawk. 597.
3 Inst. 22, 30.
2 Inst. 49.

Court may be adjourned.
2 Hawk. 24.

If the Lords agree of their Verdict that Day whether to be kept together, or go to their several Houses.
2 Hawk. 598.
And Cases ibi.

I And

Another Question was moved among them, whether the Lords who were Commissioners, to enquire of the Treason, before whom the Prisoner was indicted upon the Commission of Oyer and Terminer, might be Peers on the Tryal; and agreed by all that they might.

<small>Lords before whom the Indictment is found, may be Peers on the Tryal.</small>

If *A.* hath Malice against *B.* and meeteth him and striketh him, and then *B.* draweth at *A.* and flyeth back until he come to a Wall, and then kills *B.* this is Murder, notwithstanding his flying to the Wall; for the craft of flying shall not excuse the Malice which he had, nor shall any such Device to wreak his Malice on another, and think to be excused by Law, avail him any thing, but in such Case the Malice is enquirable, and if that be found by the Jury, then his flight is so far from excusing the Crime, that it aggravates it, *vide Cromp Just.* 22. *b. Fitz Cor.* 287. *vide at the end of that Case, in Fitz Abridgment, Coron.* 287. the Jurors were amerced for putting an under Value upon the Goods of a man who killed another in his own defence.*

<small>1 Hawk. 113, 123.

Murder notwithstanding flying to a Wall. Post. 278.

Jury undervalue Goods forfeited they are amerceable.</small>

At a Goal Delivery at *Newgate*, 11th *July* 18 *Car.* 2. *Tho. Johnson, John Girling,* and *Elizabeth Powell* were indicted for breaking the House of *Thomas Powell* (his Wife then being in the house) and stealing away above 60 *l.* in Money. Upon the Evidence the Case was, that *Powell* kept an *Ale-house,* and *Eliz. Powell* was his Servant, and had seen her Mistress put Money into a Trunk in her *Chamber*, which was 2 pair of Stairs high and locked her Trunk; and this Servant combined with the two Men to Rob her of the Money, and in order thereunto, those two Men came into the House to Drink, and found fault with all the Rooms below Stairs, and so were had up two pair of Stairs, the next Chamber to that where the Money was, and the Maid came to them, and they broke up the Trunk, and took away above 60 *l.* in Money, and upon this Evidence, myself, and my Brother *Twisden*, and Brother *Wylde* being present, were of Opinion that to take away Clergy, there must be an actual breaking of the House. For if one come into a

<small>*Johnson, Girling,* and *Powell*'s Case.</small>

---

* As this is cited, it might be imagined that in every Case of Homicide, *se defendendo,* a Man forfeited all his Goods, otherwise, why was the Jury charged with the Value of them, or amerced for their Misbehaviour, with regard to the Appraisment? But Fitzherbert goeth farther into the true State of the Case: The Defendant after he killed the Assailant fled for it. Ideo saith the Book, Catalla ejus conficantur profuga. See Foster C. L. 286.

Tavern

Tavern, or an *Ale-houſe*, and take any thing, the Law maketh them Treſpaſſers *ab initio*; and ſo if they ſteal any thing, it is Felony; yet this doth not make an actual breaking of the Houſe; but in that Caſe, if they being in the Houſe break open any Chamber-door and ſteal Goods, this is an actual breaking of the Houſe, and taketh away Clergy; but the breaking open a Trunk or Box which is locked, and ſtealing any thing out of it, is no actual breaking of the Houſe, becauſe the Trunk or Box are no part of the Houſe. But if they break open any thing which is fixed to the Free-hold, as a Cupboard Door in a Wall, &c. this is an actual breaking of the Houſe; and accordingly in the principal Caſe, the Men had there Clergy.

What ſhall be a breaking of a Houſe to take away Clergy.
2 Hawk. 497.
Vide Foſt. 108, 109.

At a Goal-delivery at Newgate, 25 *April*, 1666. 18 *Car.* 2. upon an indictment of Murder againſt *Hopkin Huggett*, a ſpecial Verdict was found to this Effect. We find that *John Berry*, and two others with him the Day and Place in the Inquiſition had *de facto*, but without Warrant (for ought appears to us) impreſſed a Man whoſe Name is not yet known, to ſerve in his Majeſties Service in the wars againſt the *Dutch Nation*; that thereupon, after the unknown man was impreſſed, he with the ſaid *John Berry*, went together quietly into *Cloth-fair*; and the ſaid *Hopkin Huggett* and three others, walking together in the *Rounds* in *Smithfield*, and ſeeing the ſaid *Berry* and two others with the man impreſſed, going into *Cloth-fair*, inſtantly purſued after them, and overtaking *Berry* and the impreſt man, and the two other Men required to ſee their Warrant, and *Berry* ſhewed them a Paper which *Hopkin Huggett* and the 3 others ſaid was no Warrant; and immediately the ſaid *H. Huggett* and the three others drew their Swords to reſcue the ſaid man Impreſt, and did thruſt at the ſaid *John Berry*; and thereupon the ſaid *John Berry* and the two others with him did draw their Swords and fight together, and thereupon the ſaid *H. Huggett* did give the Wound in the Inquiſition to the ſaid *John Berry*, whereof he inſtantly died; and if upon the whole matter, the ſaid *H. Huggett* be guilty of Murder they find ſo; If of Manſlaughter they find ſo, &c. All the Judges of *England* being met together, at *Serjeant's-Inn* in *Fleet-ſtreet*, upon other Occaſions, (and before that time, having Copies of this

Hopkin Huggett's Caſe for killing a Man
1 Lord Raym. 143.
1 H.P.C. 46.
Foſt. 138, 154.
314.

Judges differ, if Murder or Manſlaughter.

ſpecial

special Verdict sent unto them) after the other business dispatched, they were desired to give their Opinions in this Case, whether they held it to be Murder or Manslaughter. And the Lord Chief Justice *Bridgman*, Lord Chief Baron *Hales*, my Brother *Atkins*, Brother *Tyrell*, Brother *Turner*, Brother *Browne*, Brother *Archer*, and Brother *Rainsford*, having had the Notes of the Special Verdict three days before, delivered their Opinion as then advised; but they said they would not be bound by it: that this was no Murder, but only Manslaughter; and they said, that if a man be unduly arrested or restrained of his Liberty by three men, altho' he be quiet himself, and do not endeavour any Rescue, yet this is a Provocation to all other men of *England*, not only his Friends but Strangers also for common Humanity sake, as my Lord *Bridgman* said, to endeavour his Rescue; and if in such endeavour of Rescue they kill any one, this is not Murder, but only Manslaughter. And my Brother *Browne* seemed to rely on a Case in *Coke* 12. *Rep. p.* 87. where divers men were playing at Bowls, and two of them fell out and quarrelled, one with another, and a third man who had no Quarrel, in revenge of his Friend struck the other with a Bowl, of which blow he died, this was held to be only Manslaughter. But myself, Brother *Twisden*, Brother *Wyndham*, and Brother *Morton*, were of another Opinion; and we held it to be a Murder, because there was (as we thought) no provocation at all. And if one man assault another without Provocation, and kill him, this is Murder; the Law in that Case implying Malice. And we find it was resolved by all the Judges in the Lord *Morley's Case*, that no Words, be they what they will, were such a Provocation in Law, as if upon them one kills another would diminish or lessen the Offence from being Murder, to be but Manslaughter. As if one called another Son of a Whore, and giveth him the Lie, and upon those Words the other kill him that gave the Words, this notwithstanding those Words, is Murder; and we thought those Words were apter to provoke a man to kill another, than the bare seeing a man to be unduly pressed when the Party pressed willingly renders himself. But we held that

(60)

1 Hawk. 129 *.
Cromp. 27.
Lord Raym.
1296.
Holt. 4ᶜ 5.

Vide Lord *Morly's* Case.
Ante 55 *.

* The Principles on which this Case was ruled, are controverted by Mr. J. Foster, 315 to 318.

such

such a provocation as must take off the killing of a man from Murder to be but Manslaughter, must be some open Violence, or actual striving with, or striking one another; and that answers the Case cited by my Brother *Browne*. For there it must be intended that the two men that fell out were actually fighting together; for if there passed only Words betwixt these Two, and upon them, a third Person struck one of them with a Bowl, and killed him, we held that to be Murder. And to this my Lord *Bridgman* and the other Judges agreed, and we thought the Case in question to be much the stronger, because the Party himself who was impressed was quiet, and made no Resistance, and they who medled were no Friends of his, or Acquaintance, but were Strangers, and did not so much as desire them which had him in Custody to let him go, but presently without more ado, drew their Swords at them, and ran at them. And we thought it to be of dangerous Consequence to give any Encouragement to private men to take upon themselves to be the Assertors of other Men's Liberties, and to become Patrons to rescue them from Wrong; especially in a Nation where good Laws are for the Punishment of all such Injuries, and one great end of Law is to right Men by peaceable Means, and to discountenance all Endeavours to right themselves, much less other Men by Force.

Secondly, We four were of Opinion, that if *A.* assault *B.* without any Provocation, and draw his Sword at him, and run at him; and then *B.* to defend himself draw his Sword, and they fight together: If *A.* kill *B.* it is Murder, and *B.* drawing his Sword to defend himself shall not lessen the Offence of *A.* from being Murder, to be Manslaughter only: And to this the other Judges did (as I take it) agree. For it were unreasonable, that if one Man draw upon another, and run at him without any Provocation that the other Man should stand still, and not defend himself, and it is also unreasonable that his endeavour to defend himself should lessen the Offence of him who set upon him without Provocation.

1 Hawk. 125.
Fost. 295.
Lord Raym. 1493.
2 Roll. 461.

But we four held, that if two men be quarrelling, and actually fighting together, and another Man runneth in to aid one of them and kill the other, this is but Manslaughter, because there was an actual fighting and striving with violence.

1 Hawk. 129.

So

So we held, If such People who are called Spirits take up a Youth, or other Person to carry him away, and thereupon there is a Tumult raised, and several Persons run in, and there is a Man killed in the Fray, this is but Manslaughter: For there is an open Affray, and actual Force, which is a suddain Provocation, and so that Death which ensueth is but Manslaughter. But where People are at Peace, there if another Man upon Suspicion that an Injury is done to one of them, will assault and kill him whom he thinketh did the Injury, this is Murder, so that we hold nothing but an open Affray or striving can be a Provocation to any Person to meddle with an Injury done to another, if in that medling he kill a Man, to diminish or lessen the Offence from Murder to Manslaughter.

Memorandum, After this Difference I granted a *Cerciorari* to remove the Cause into the King's Bench, to be argued there, and to receive a final and legal Determination; and altho' all the Judges of the Court were clearly of Opinion that it was Murder, yet it being in Case of Life, we did not think it prudent to give him Judgment of Death, but admitted him to his Clergy; and after he read, and was burned in the Hand, we ordered him to lie in Prison eleven Months without Bail, and afterwards until he found Sureties to be of the good Behaviour during his Life.

Caffy and *Cotter's* Case.

Robbery and Burglary by Fraud.
1 H. P.C. 552.

Vide Cok. Pl. Cor. 64. pretence of Huy and Cry.

At the Goal-Delivery in the *Old Baily,* 10 *Oct.* 1666. *Tho. Caffy,* and *John Cotter,* were indicted for robbing *William Pinkney,* a Goldsmith by the *Templebar,* in his House near the High-way in the Night Time, and stealing several parcels of Plate, and other Things from him. And they were also indicted for the same Offence for Burglary for breaking his House in the Night, and stealing his Plate, &c. and on both these Indictments they were arraigned and tryed, and upon the Evidence the Case appeared to be that *Cotter* was a Lodger in the House of the said *Pinkney,* and knowing that he had Plate and Money to a good Value, he combined with the aforesaid *Caffy,* and one *John Harrington,* and *Gerrard Cleashard,* and

and they three contrived that one of those three should come as Servant of the other to hire Lodgings there, for his Master and another Gentleman; and *Cotter* told them, that *Pinkney* was one who constantly kept Prayers every Night, and they could not have so good an Opportunity to surprize him as to desire to join in Prayer with him, and at that time to fall on him and his Maid, there being then no other Company in the House; and accordingly one of them came on *Saturday* in the Afternoon, and hired Lodgings there, pretending it to be for his Master and another Gentleman of good Quality, and about eight o'Clock at night, they all came thither, two of them being in very good Habit, and when they were in their Chamber they sent for Ale, and desired *Pinkney* to drink with them, which he did; and while they were drinking, *Cotter* came in to his Lodging, and they hearing one go up Stairs, asked who it was, and *Pinkney* told them it was an honest Gentleman, one Mr. *Cotter*, who lodged in his House, and they desired to be acquainted with him, and that he might be desired to come to them; and thereupon *Pinkney* sent his Maid to him to let him know the Gentlemen desired to be acquainted with him, to which *Cotter* sent word it was late, the next day was the Sabbath, and he desired to be private, and thereupon those Persons told *Pinkney* they had heard he was a Religious Man, and used to perform Family Duties, in which they desired to join with him. At which *Pinkney* was very well pleased that he had got such Religious Persons, and so called to Prayers, and while he was at his Devotion they rose up, and bound him and his Servant, and then *Cotter* came to them, and shewed them where his Money and Plate lay, and they ransacked the House, and broke open several Doors and Cupboards fixed to the House, and upon this Evidence, myself, my Brother *Wylde*, Recorder, and Mr. *Howell*, Deputy Recorder, being all who were there present of the Long Robe, were of Opinion that the Entrance into his House being gained by Fraud, with an intent to rob, and they making use of this Entrance, thus fraudulently obtained as in the Night Time to break open Doors, &c. this was Burglary, agreeable to the Case of *Farr* in this Book, and the Case of Mr. *Lemott*, in this Book, and accordingly they were found guilty, and had Judgment, and were executed.

1 Hawk. 161.
And Cases cited, ibid.

Ante 43.
Ante 42.

At

Grey's Case for killing his Apprentice. Poft. 133. 1 H.P.C. 454, 474. Foft. 262.

At the same Sessions *John Grey* being indicted for the Murder of *William Golding*, the Jury found a special Verdict to this Effect, viz. We find that the Day, Year, and Place in the Indictment mentioned, *John Grey*, the Prisoner was a *Blacksmith*, and that *William Golding*, the Person killed was his Servant, and that *Grey*, his Master, commanded him to mend certain Stamps, being Part belonging to his Trade, which he neglected to do; and the said *Grey*, his Master, after coming in asked him the said *Golding*, why he had not done it, and the said *Grey* told the said *Golding*, that if he would not serve him, he should serve in *Bridewel*, to which the said *Golding* replied, that he had as good serve in *Bridewel* as serve the said *Grey* his Master; whereupon the said *Grey*, without any other Provocation, struck the said *Golding* with a Bar of Iron, which the said *Grey* then had in his Hand, upon which he and *Golding* were working at the *Anvil*, and with the said blow he broke his Skull, of which he died; and if this be Murder, &c. This Case was found specially by the Desire of my Brother *Wylde*, and I shewed the special Verdict to all my Brethren, Judges of the King's Bench, and to my Lord *Bridgman* Chief Justice of the Common Pleas. And we were all of Opinion that this was Murder. For if a Father, Master, or Schoolmaster, will correct his Child, Servant, or Scholar, they must do it with such Things as are fit for Correction, and not with such Instruments as may probably kill them. For otherwise, under pretence of Correction, a Parent might kill his Child, or a Master his Servant, or a Schoolmaster his Scholar, and a Bar of Iron is no Instrument for Correction. It is all one as if he had run him through with a Sword; and my Brother *Morton* said he remembered a Case at *Oxford* Assizes before Justice *Jones*, then Judge of Assize, where a *Smith* being chiding with his Servant, upon some cross Answer given by his Servant, he having a piece of hot Iron in his Hand, run it into his Servants Belly, and it was judged Murder, and the Party executed. And my Lord *Bridgman* said, that in his Circuit there was a Woman indicted for murdering her

Vide Dalton Juft 218. a case cited before Justice *Walmsly*, 43 El. At *Stafford* Assizes, where on Words 'twixt Husband and Wife, he suddainly struck her with a Pestle and killed her, and it was adjudged Murder; yet a Husband by Law may correct, but the Pestle was not an Instrument to correct withal *.
1 H.P.C. 457 Crompt. 120.?.

* There are various Editions of Dalton, and the Paging differs in most, this is Chap. 93. and here Dalton puts a Quære to this Case, cited in the Margin by the learned Editor, " Why it should " be Murder, considering there appeareth no precedent Malice, " and that it was done upon the sudden and upon Provocation?" But Dalton does not seem in this Quære to have well understood the true legal meaning of the Word *Malice*, which is well defended by Foster 256, 257.

Child,

Child, and it appeared upon the Evidence, that she cicked her and stamped upon her Belly, and he judged it Murder: And my Brother *Twisden* said, he ruled such a Case formerly in *Gloucester* Circuit, for a piece of Iron or a Sword, or a great Cudgel, with which a Man probably may be slain, are not Instruments of Correction. And therefore when a Master strikes his Servant willingly with such Things as those are, if Death ensue, the Law shall judge it Malice prepensed, and therefore the Statute of 5 *H.* 4. *c.* 5. which enacts, that if any one does cut out the Tongue, or put out the Eyes of any of the King's Subjects of Malice prepensed, it shall be Felony. If a Man do cut out the Tongue of another Man voluntarily, the Law judgeth it of *Malice prepensed.* And so where one Man killeth another without any Provocation, the Law judgeth it Malice prepensed; and in the Lord *Morley*'s Case in this Book, it was resolved by all the Judges, that Words are no Provocation to lessen the Offence from being Murder, if one Man kill another upon ill Words given to him. But if a Parent, Master, or Schoolmaster, correct his Child, Servant, or Scholar, with such Things as are usual and fit for Correction, and they happen to die, *Poulton de pace, page* 120. saith this is by Misadventure, and cites for Authority, *Kelloway* 103, *a, b, &* 136, *a.* But that Book which puts this Case in *Kelloway* is 136, *a.* saith, that if a Man correct his Servant, or Lord his Villain, and by force of that Correction he dieth, although he did not intend to kill him, yet this is Felony, because they ought to govern themselves in their Correction in such Ways that such a Misadventure might not happen. And I suppose, because the Word Misadventure is there used, therefore *Poulton* concludeth (it may be truly) that it is but Misadventure.

Vide Coke Pl. Cor. in his Chapter for cutting out Tongues.

Ante 55.

It is but Misadventure in this Case if death ensue upon Correction, if it be with such Things as are usual to correct withal. *Vide Dalton*'s Justice of Peace, last Edition 285. Books cited to this Purpose. H. P. C. 12.

And in this Principal Case, upon Certificate, many Persons of good Commendation of the general esteem that *Grey* had, I did certifie the King, that though in strictness of Law, his Offence was Murder; yet it was attended with such Circumstances as might render the Person an Object of his Majesty's Grace and Pardon, he having a very good Report among all his own Company of his own Trade, and of all his Neighbours, and upon this the King was pleased to grant him his Pardon.

1 Hawk. 111.
t H. P. C. 454.
473, 474.
c Mod. 287.
Fost. 262.
Cowp. 262.

Tomson's Case.
1 Hawk. 127,
128 in notis.
8 Mod. 164.
12 Mod. 629.
But vide 12
Mod. 256.

One slain in endeavouring to part two fighting where it is Murder.

At the Sessions in the *Old Bailey* holden after *Hilary Term, Caroli Secundi, Thomas Tomson* was indicted for murdering of *Allen Dawes*, and the Jury found a special Verdict to this Effect, viz. that the Day, Year, and Place in the Indictment mentioned, *Thomas Tomson* the Prisoner and his Wife, were fighting in the House of the said *Allen Dawes*, who was killed, and the said *Allen Dawes* seeing them fighting, came in and endeavoured to part them, and thereupon the said *Tomson* thrust away the said *Dawes*, and threw him down upon a piece of Iron, which was a Bar in a Chimney, which kept up the Fire, and by that one of the Ribs of the said *Dawes* was broken, of which he died; and if the Court judge this Murder, they find so, or if Manslaughter, then they find so.

1 Hawk. 128.
Fost. 310.

And I put this Case to my Lord Chief Justice Baron *Hales* and my Brother, and some other of my Brethren, and we all agreed as it is resolved in *Young*'s Case, Co. 4. Report, and also in *Mackally*'s Case, Co. 9. Report, that if upon a suddain Affray, a Constable or Watchman or any that come in aid of them, who endeavour to part them, are killed, this is Murder; and we hold likewise, that if no Constable or Watchman be there, if any other

Vide Lambert Fitzherbert
Fol. 262. *Dyer* 128.
1 Hawk. 127, 8.
1 Hawk. 127.
Fost. 272.

Person come to part them, and he be killed, this is Murder: For every one in such Case is bound to aid and preserve the King's Peace. But in all those Cases it is necessary that the Party who was fighting and killed him that came to part them, did know or had Notice given, that they came for that Purpose. As for the Constable or other Person who cometh to part them, to charge them in the King's Name to keep the King's Peace, by which they have Notice of their Intents; for otherwise if two are fighting, and a Stranger runs in with Intent to part them, yet the Party who is fighting, may think he cometh in Aid of the other with whom he is fighting, unless some such Notice be given as aforesaid, that he was a Constable, and came to part them: And that appeareth by *Mackally*'s Case before cited, where in case of an Arrest by a Serjeant, it is necessary to make it Murder that the Serjeant tell him that he doth Arrest, for else if he doth say nothing, but fall upon the Man and be killed by him, this

is but Manslaughter, nnless it appear that the Person ar- | 1 Hawk. 128.
rested did know him to be a Serjeant, and that he came
to arrest him; for as the Case is there put, if one seeing
the Sheriff or a Serjeant whom he knoweth hath a Warrant to arrest him, and to prevent it before the Officer
come so near as to let him know he doth arrest him, he
Shoots again at him, and kills him, this is Murder; and in
the principal Case though the Jury find that *Dawes* came
to part the Man and Wife, yet it doth not appear whether
it is found that *Tomson* knew his Intent, nor that *Dawes*
spake any Words whereby he might understand his Intention, as charging them to keep the King's Peace, &c. 8 Mod. 164.
And so we held it to be only Manslaughter, which in Law Fost. 275.
is properly chance-medley, that is where one Man upon
a suddain Occasion kills another with Malice in Fact, or
Malice implied by Law.

If a Person in the Night Time break a House, and steal Burglary, tho'
Goods, this is Burglary, though no Person be at that Time no Person be
in the House. So if a Man hath two Houses, one in the 1 Hawk. 160.
City and another in the Country, and while he is in the Ante 52.
one House the other is broken open, no body being in it,
and Goods stolen, this is Burglary, *Popham's Reports* 42
and 512 by all the Judges.

A Servant in the House lodging in a Room remote from Burglary by a
his Master in the Night Time, draweth the Latch of a Servant in his
Door to come into his Master's Chamber, with an intent to House, draw-
kill him, this on a special Verdict agreed by all the Judges ing a Latch
to be Burglary. of a Door is
actual break-
ing an House. 1 Hawk. 160, 161, 162.

Note, That in *Popham's* Report's 84. In one *Baynes's* To make a
Case, it is said, that the said *Baynes* with another coming Robbery of a
in the Night Time to a Tavern to drink, the said *Baynes* House within
stole a Cup in which they drank out, of a Chamber in the 8. cap. & 5 E.
said House, his Wife and Servant being in the said House, 6. c. 9. take
for which he was indicted and found guilty; and it is any Clergy
there reported, that by the Opinion of *Anderson, Popham,* must either be
and *Periam*, and the then Recorder and Serjeant at Law an actual
there present, it was agreed that this was no Burglary; breaking of
which certainly is good Law, because there was no actu- such a vio-
al breaking of the House, which is of necessity to make a lence to some
Person there
that they are put in fear or dread. *Vide* my Reasons for it in this Discourse, for
which I hold the last Resolution in *Baynes's* Case to be no Law. 1 Hawk. 164.
1 H. P. C. 552. 1 H. P. C. 523. 1 H. P. C. 554. Hut, 20.

Burglary. *Vide Co. Pl. Cor.* 64. But that in that Cafe of *Baynes*, it is there faid, that it was refolved by them there likewife, that that ſtealing was ſuch a Robbery for which he was oufted of the Benefit of his Clergy by the *Stat.* of 5 *E. 6 cap.* 9. and was hanged, which laſt Reſolution I hold clearly not to be Law; for that that *Statute* of 5 *Ed.* 6. *cap.* 6. is only to enlarge the *Stat.* 23 *H.* 8. *cap.* 1. which amongſt other Crimes took away Clergy from fuch Perſons who robbed any in their Houſes, their Wives, Children, or Servants being there, and put in fear or dread. Now that *Stat.* of 5 *Ed.* 6. ordained that although the Perſons who were in the Houſe, lay in fome other part of the Houſe, which was robbed, and were aſleep at the Time, and ſo did not hear the Thieves, and conſequently were not put in fear, yet that Statute taketh away Clergy in that Cafe; but notwithſtanding there muſt be a Robbery, for both the *Stat.* of 5 *Ed.* 6. and the *Stat.* of 23 *H.* 8. is againſt ſuch as ſhall rob Men in their Dwelling Houſes. Now the taking away of a Cup in which Men are drinking, as *Bayne*'s Cafe was, is only Larceny and no Robbery, for Larceny is defcribed to be a fraudulent taking away of another Man's Goods above the Value of 12*d*. with an Intent to ſteal them, *Poulton de pace* 125, *b*. and Stamford *Pl. Cor.* 24. *a*. but Robbery is defcribed to be a Rapine that is, a violent taking any thing from a Man's Perſon; and when it is applied to robbing of Houſes, there muſt be the fame circumſtance of Force *Vide Poulton de pace* 128. *Stamford Pl. Cor.* 27, *a*, *b. Co. Pl. Cor.* 68. For of neceſſity there muſt be fomething to diſtinguiſh a Robbery in a Houſe, from that which is but a mere Larceny, and that is one, *viz.* The Larceny is only fraudulent without any actual Force, and a Robbery is done with Force; and this will appear by examining the Nature of Burglary, which is the robbing of a Houſe by Night, there muſt be Force committed, as the actual breaking of a Houſe makes it Burglary: For if the Door of a Houſe be open, and a Thief enter in the Night and ſteal Goods, this is only Larceny, and no Burglary, becauſe there was no Force, which is that which diſtinguiſhed Robbery from Larceny. Now this Force, which will make a robbery of a Houſe within thoſe Statutes to take away Clergy, may either

1 Hawk. 145.

2 Hawk. 494.

be

be an actual breaking of the House, or an Assault upon the Person. And therefore if Company come to drink in a Tavern, or other Victualing-house, and being there they break open a Door of another Chamber or Cupboard in the Wall which is fixed to the Freehold, and steal away Goods, this is a Robbery, for which Clergy is taken away by those Statutes. But the breaking open a Trunk or Box, and taking away things is no Robbery of a House within the Statute, because those things which were broken were no part of the House: and so likewise it is the case of Violence offered to the Person of a Man, and taking away his Goods with force. As in case a Thief cometh into a Man's House or Shop, the Door being open, and assaults the honest Man in the House or Shop, and taketh away things by Violence, this is likewise a Robbing of a House within those Statutes, but if in those cases he had come into the House or Shop, and privately stolen away any thing, that had been only Larceny, and not Robbery: and this exposition agreeth with the sense of the Parliament in the Statute of 39 *Eliz. c.* 15. which expounds Robbing of Houses in the day time to be the actual breaking them; for all former Statutes took away Clergy where a House was robbed in the day time, some Person being then in the House; but this Statute of 39 *Eliz.* recites the mischief, because Robbing of Houses when no Person was therein, was not so penal as Robbing them when some Person was therein, and thereby had Persons took opportunity to commit many Robberies in Houses when people were gone abroad to hear Divine Service, or gone to their Labour, and declareth that, that Robbery was, *viz.* by breaking and entering into Mens Houses at such time, and enacts that such Robbing of any House, and stealing from thence Goods of the value of 5*s.* they shall not have the benefit of the Clergy, which I think is a full exposition that Robbing of Houses; in that case, must be an actual breaking, that is, an actual force committed in breaking of the House; but in the other case that I put of Robbing a Man in his House by assault upon his Person, as where a Thief enters the House or Shop of a Man without any actual breaking, the Door being open, and by Violence takes away his Goods, in that Case I conceive the Indictment must express that he did assault him

1 H. P. C. 553.

2 H. P. C. 357.
2 Hawk. 496.

And the Stat, 1 E. 6. 12. calls that breaking of Houses, which the Stat. 23 H. 8. & 5 E. 6. calls robbing of Houses, and so expounds them.

2 Hawk. 500.

1 Hawk. 149. and in notis to sect 6, same page.

2 Hawk. 494.

2 Hawk. 497. 1 H.P.C. 552. P. 68.

2 Hawk. 500.

him and put him in fear, becaufe that Circumftance is neceffary to be laid to make it a Robbery from a Man's Perfon, and therefore 5 *Eliz. Dyer* 224, *b.* One being indicted for taking of Money from the Perfon of a Man by the High-way, had his Clergy, becaufe it was not faid that he was put in fear, and the Book faith *quod non eft robberia* if the Perfon be not put in fear, although Goods be taken from his Perfon; and for that Caufe was the Statute of 8 *Eliz. cap.* 4. made to take away Clergy from him who privily taketh away any Money or Goods from the Perfon of a Man. If Thieves come in-to a Houfe by Night, the Door being open, and take away Goods, this is no Burglary, as hath been faid be-fore. But in that cafe, if they put any in the Houfe in fear and dread, and take away Goods, I hold this to be robbery of a Houfe, for which the Thieves are oufted of Clergy by the Statute of 23 *H.* 8. *cap.* 7. If the in-dictment be laid, that they put thofe in the Houfe in fear and dread, and that be proved upon the Evidence.

Meffenger, Appletree, Bafely, Green, and others in-dicted for le-vying War and pulling down Bawdy-houfes, and breaking open Prifons. 2 St. Tr. 581. 1 H.P.C. 134. Poft. 215.

Memorandum, That at the Seffions at the *Old Bailey,* after *Eafter* in the twentieth Year of King *Charles* the 2d. Several diffolute Perfons having on *Eafter* Tuefday and Wednefday next before affembled together, and led by Perfons whom they called Captains, and having Co-lours, *viz.* Aprons, *&c.* on Staves, went to feveral places on pretence to pull down Bawdy-houfes, and break open Prifons and fet Prifoners at Liberty, and having actually pulled down fome Houfes, and broke up the Prifon at *Clerkenwell,* and let out four Prifoners there, were by the direction of the King's Councel, *viz.* Mr. *Attorney,* Sir *Jeffery Palmer,* having Order to pro-ceed againft them profecuted, he directed four indictments to be preferred againft them, who were taken, *viz.* one indictment againft *Peter Meffenger, Richard Bafely, Wil-liam Green,* and *Thomas Appletree,* and another indict-ment againft *Edward Cotton,* and a third againft *Edward Bedell* and *Richard Lattimer,* and a fourth againft *Tho-mas Limerick.* All the Indictments were, that they with other Perfons to the number of 500, unknown to the Jurors, being armed in a War-like manner with Swords, half Pikes, Halberts, long Staves and other Arms Of-fenfive and Defenfive, with Force and Arms unlawfully, and

and traiteroufly affembled themfelves together, and levied War againft the King, &c. and firft I told them they had not done well to make fo many feveral indictments, for by that means the King's Evidence would be broken, whereas if all had been put into one indictment, the Evidence as to the main Defign would have been intire againft all, and then the affembling in feveral places to the fame intent had made the matter more foul, and would have been aptly given in Evidence againft them all to the fame Jury, and the feveral Acts which each of them did, would have come in better; but however we proceeded upon the indictments as they were, and after the Evidence given againft the four in the firft indictment, when I came to give Directions to the Jury, I told them that although I was well fatisfied in my own Judgment, that fuch affembling together as was proved, and the pulling down of Houfes upon pretence they were Bawdy-houfes, was High-Treafon, becaufe they took upon them regal Power to reform that which belonged to the King by his Law and Juftices to correct and reform: and it would be a ftrange way and mifchievous to all People to have fuch a rude rabble without an indictment to proceed in that manner againft all Perfons Houfes which they would call Bawdy-houfes, for then no Man were fafe, therefore as that way tore the Government out of the King's Hands, fo it deftroyed the great privilege of the People, which is not to be proceeded againft, but upon an indictment firft found by a Grand Jury, and after upon a legal Tryal by another Jury where the Party accufed was heard to make his defence; yet I told them, becaufe the Kings of this Nation had oftentimes been fo merciful as when fuch Outrages had been heretofore done not to proceed capitally againft the Offenders, but to proceed againft the Offenders in the Star-Chamber, being willing to reduce their People by milder ways if it were poffible to their Duty and Obedience; yet that lenity of the King in fome Cafes did not hinder the King when he faw there was need to proceed in a feverer way, to take that courfe which was warranted by Law, and to make greater Examples, that the People may know the Law, is not wanting fo far to the fafety of the King and his People, as to let fuch Outrages

rages go without capital punishment, which is at this time absolutely necessary, because we ourselves have seen a Rebellion raised by gathering People together upon fairer Pretences than this was, for no such Persons use at first to declare their wickedest Design, but when they see that they may effect their Design, then they will not stick to go further, and give the Law themselves, and destroy all that oppose them: but yet because there was no body of the Long Robe there but my Brother *Wylde*, then Recorder of *London*, and myself, and that this Example might have the greater Authority, I did resolve that the Jury should find the matter Specially, and then I would procure a meeting of all the Judges of *England*, and what was done should be by their Opinion, that so this Question might have such a Resolution as no Person afterwards should have reason to doubt the Law, and all Persons might be warned how they for the time to come mingle themselves with such Rabble on any kind of such Pretences, and thereupon the Jury as to the first four in the first indictment gave a Special Verdict to this Effect, *viz.*

A Special Verdict as to *Messenger, Appletree, Basely* and *Green*.

They find that the 24*th of March* last, a great number of Persons to the number mentioned in the Indictment were assembled together in *East Smithfield* and *Moorfields* in the County of *Middlesex* with Arms mentioned in the Indictment, on pretence of pulling down Bawdy-houses, that *Basely* led them, and was called their Captain, and had in his Hand a naked Sword which he brandished over his Head, and that *Messenger* had a piece of green Apron on a Staff; which he flourished as Colours in the Head of the Company, and that *Basely*, and he led the Company as their Leaders; that they did the like on Wednesday the 25*th* of *March*, and were breaking down Houses. That *Peverell*, one of the Constables of *Middlesex*, having a Constable's Staff in his hand, came to them with other Persons to aid him, and charged them to depart and keep the Peace, and thereupon, *Basely* with his Sword struck him, and wounded him, and several Persons assembled with him, struck him down, and took away his Constables Staff. That the said *William Green* was among them casting up his Cap, and hollowing with a Staff in his Hand, and that whilst he was amongst them he was knocked Down by a Party of the King's Soldiers

that

that came to suppress them, and was then taken. That *Basely* struck at the Ensign that led those Soldiers: that the said *Appletree* was among them both Days, and was the first that struck at *Peverell* the Constable, and was amongst them at *Burlingham*'s House at *Saffronhill* in the County of *Middlesex*, and pulled part of the House down, and the next House to it, and struck at one that admonished him to be quiet. And if on the whole matter, it shall seem to the Court that they are guilty of the Offence mentioned in the Indictment, then they find them Guilty, &c.

On the 2d. Indictment as to *Cotton* alone, the Jury did find that at the time and place mentioned in the Indictment, a great number of Persons, to the number mentioned in the Indictment, met together armed with Swords, Clubs, Staves and other Weapons, under pretence of pulling down Bawdyhouses, and had a Cloth on a Staff for an Ensign carried before them. And that *Sir Philip Howard*, with a Troop of the King's Guard, found them armed in such seditious manner, and commanded them to disperse, that they refused so to do, and threw Stones at him, that some of them enquired who it was that led those Guards, whether it was the Duke of *York*, and being told it was, they presently threw Stones at *Sir P. H.* who led the Horse, and some of them said that unless the King would give them liberty of Conscience, *May-Day* should be a bloody day, others did Kill the Guards, and others said, that they would come and pull down *Whitehall*, and others said they would be with them at *Whitehall*, (the King's Capital Palace) and that they cared not for the Guards, for they were but 2 or 300, and they could easily knock them on the Head; that they continued many Hours till they were dispersed by the Guards. That *Cotton* who was indicted, was one of them assembled in this manner, and that *Cotton* was amongst them the next day when they were assembled in the same manner, and was pulling down a House in the Parish of *St. Leonard Shoreditch* in the County of *Middlesex*; and if on the whole matter, &c.

On the third Indictment against *Bedell* and *Lattimer*, the Jury find that the day and place mentioned in the Indictment, a great number of Persons to the number mentioned

Special Verdict also as to *Cotton*. 2 St. Tr. 591.

Special Verdict on the third Indictment. *Bedel* and *Lattimer*. 2 St. Tr. 591.

mentioned in the Indictment armed as in the Indictment, did meet together in *Clerkenwell Green* in the County of *Middlesex*, on pretence of breaking open Prisons, and releasing Prisoners; that one of them who had a half Pike in his Hand, owned himself to be their Captain; that they came so assembled together to a Place there called the New Prison, being a publick Prison of the County of *Middlesex*, and then and there said, that they came to search for Prisoners, and break open the Prison Doors, and let out four Prisoners, two whereof were committed thither for Felony, and two for other Offences, and that they being charged to depart, replied, they had been Servants long, but now they would be Masters; that some being taken, they cried one die and all die: That *Lattimer* was amongst them, and active in breaking of the Prison, and was with the rest in the Prison after it was broken open; And that *Bedell* was there, and being pursued by one of the King's Soldiers, called out to the rest of the Company to face about, and not to leave him, and if on the Whole, &c.

Special Verdict as to Lymerick. 2 St. Tr. 591.

On the fourth Indictment against *Lymerick*, the Jury find that the Day, Year, and Place in the Indictment mentioned, a great number of Persons to the number, &c. assembled together on pretence of pulling down of Bawdy-houses, and being armed *prout* in the Indictment, they marched in warlike Manner, and the said *Lymerick* led them as their Captain with a Club in his Hand, and was owned by the Company to be their Captain: That the said *Lymerick* had the said Persons to the House of *Peter Burlingham*, and they pulled down the said House, and destroyed and took away divers Goods of the said *Burlingham*'s to the value of 30*l*. And if on the whole Matter, &c.

And in *Easter* Term following, all the Judges met at my Chamber, there being then but eleven. My Lord *Bridgeman*, who was Chief Justice of the Common Pleas being then Lord *Keeper*, the Judges were myself, Chief Justice of the King's Bench, Sir *M. Hales* the Chief Baron, and my Brother *Atkins*, Brother *Twisden*, Brother *Tyrell*, Brother *Turner*, Brother *Wyndham*, Brother *Archer*, Brother *Rainsford*, Brother *Morton*, and Brother *Wylde*.

And

And on the whole Matter the Chief Baron *Hales* delivered his Opinion, that there was no Treason in the Case, because he said that the *Stat.* Q. *Mary, cap.* 12. is, that if any Persons to the number of Twelve or more assemble to the Intent to pull down Enclosures, &c. with Force, and continue together an Hour after Proclamation made for their departure it shall be Felony, and if those Actions had been Treason at Common Law, it had been to no Purpose to make it Felony.

1 Hawk. 554. 1 H P C 134. The Reasons of Hales Opinion in this Case. 1 H.P.C. 131. 2 St. Tr. 593.

But all the other Judges answered, that this was the Objection made by some Judges in the Case of *Bradshaw* and *Burton*, which is reported by *Popham* in his Reports, *p.* 122. And there it was resolved, that if any Persons assembled with Force to alter the Laws, or to set a price on Victuals, or to lay violent Hands on the Magistrate as on the Mayor of *London* and the Like, and with Force attempt to put the same in Exceution, this is a Rebellion and Treason at the Common Law; and they there resolved that the Statute of 1 *Mary* was to be intended where Persons to the number of Twelve or more pretending any or all of them to be injured in particular, as by Reason of their common or other Interest in the Land inclosed, and the Like, assemble to pull it down forcibly in Cases where they have an Interest, or where in particular, they are annoyed or grieved, that is no Treason: But in case their Act goeth generally to pull down Inclosures in which they, or any of them are not particularly concerned, this Act if it be put in Execution by force is Treason at Common Law. And it was agreed by us all, that the *Stat.* of 13 *Eliz.* which maketh the Intention in many cases Treason, extends to nothing, but where if the Act had been done it had been Treason at the Common Law.

2 St. Tr. 593.

And therefore all the rest of the Judges did unanimously agree that this rising with Intent to pull down Bawdyhouses in general, or to break open Prisons in general, and let out Prisoners, and putting their Intention in Execution by Force, any of these Instances was a levying

2 St. Tr. 593.

War

War against the King, and High Treason at Common Law within the Declaration of the *Stat.* of 25 *Ed.* 3. And for that, besides the Resolution in *Popham*'s Reports before cited, we considered the Case of the Apprentices reported in the second Part of *Anderson*'s Reports, *p.* 4 and 5. where it was resolved that by the Statute of 13 *Eliz.* If any intend to levy War for any Thing which the Queen by her Laws and Justice ought to do, and reform in Government as Queen, this shall be an intendment to levy War against the Queen within that Statute of 13 *Eliz.* And as we said before, nothing can be Treason by the Intention within the Statute which had not been Treason by the Common Law, if it had been actually put in Execution. And see the same Book of *Anderson* second

Pl. 49.

Part 66, and by the case of several Persons in *Oxfordshire* rising to pull down Inclosures in general, resolved accordingly, in which Case it was also resolved, that if any Persons rise and assemble together, with intent to levy War, the Justices of the Peace and Sheriffs may use Force to suppress such Rebels without any special Commission or Warrant, and this by the Common Law: And see *Popham*'s Reports 121, and a Resolution of all the

3. H. 7. 1. 10.
Popham 121.
1 Hawk. 298.
2 St. Tr. 594.

Judges, 39 *Eliz.* that any Justice of the Peace, Sheriff, or other Magistrate, or any other Subject of the King may by the Common Law arm themselves to suppress Riots, Rebellions, or resist Enemies and endeavour themselves to suppress such disturbers of the Peace: But they said the most discreet Way was for every one to attend and assist the Justices in such Case, or other Ministers of the King in doing of it, and *Cook Pl. Cor.* 9. If any levy War to expulse Strangers, to deliver Men out of Prison, to remove Councellors, or to any other and pretending Reformation on their own Heads without Warrant, this is a levying of War against the King, because they took upon them Royal Authority. And *Moor*'s Reports,

1 St. Tr. 197.

p. 620, 621. in the Case of the Earl of *Essex*, in which amongst other Things it was resolved, that his attempt with Force to remove the Queen's Councellors was High Treason, and likewise that the Earl of *Southampton*, who adhered to him, although he knew of no other purpose of the Earl of *Essex*, but a private Quarrel against some of the Queen's Servants, yet this was Treason in him,

the

the Act of the Earl of *Essex* being Rebellion and Treason, and so it was also resolved, that all those who went with him out of *Essex-house* in aid of him, it was Treason in them, whether they knew any thing of his Intent or not, and *Cro. 1st part p.* 583. In *Benstad's* Case, it was resolved by all the Judges, that going to Lambeth-house in Warlike Manner with Drums, and a Multitude as in the Indictment, to the Number of 300, to surprize the *Arch-Bishop*, who was a Privy Councellor, was Treason. And 2*dly*, it was resolved that the Justices of *Oyer* and *Terminer*, may sit, enquire and try Prisoners all in one Day. 3*dly*. It was resolved, that the breaking of a Prison wherein Traitors were in durance, and causing them to escape, was Treason, although the Parties did not know that Traitors were there. And so to break a Prison whereby Felons escape, this is Felony, though they do not know them to be in Prison for such Offence, *Note,* That Resolution as to breaking a Prison where Felons, *&c.* are, must (as I think) be intended only where the Intent was only to break open one Prison and no more, for if the Design was to break open Prisons in general, and they put that in Execution as to one Prison, that is High Treason according to the Books before cited; but then on the Evidence it must be proved that their Intent was such, and by such proof as satisfieth the Jury.

Cro. Car.
1 Jones 455.
S. C.

Cro. Car. 583.
Cro. Jac. 404.
Cro. Car. 448. con.

After this Resolution in general, we went to consider the particular Cases as they were found upon the several special Verdicts; and thereupon it was agreed by all of us, except the Chief Baron, who said he doubted on the Main, that as to *Messenger* and *Basely* in the first Verdict, and to *Cotton* in the second special Verdict; and as to *Lymerick* in the fourth special Verdict, that the Matter as was found against these four, was High Treason in them all, and accordingly they had Judgment, and were executed: But as to *Appletree* in the first special Verdict; and as to *Lattimer* in the third special Verdict, there was difference in Opinion amongst us, whether

2 St. Tr. 594.

whether the Verdict was sufficiently found against them to judge it High Treason or not. For besides the Chief Baron who was against all, my Brother *Atkyns*, *Tyrell*, *Wyndham*, and *Wylde*, held that the Verdict was not sufficient against those two for to give Judgment that they were guilty of Treason, because they said it was not expresly found, that they were aiding and assisting: But myself, Brother *Turner*, *Twisden*, *Archer*, *Raynsford*, and *Moreton*, thought the Verdict as it was found against them to be as full and plain as any of the Rest. For first as to *Appletree*, the Verdict first finds in general, that the Number in the Indictment were assembled, as in the Indictment, with an Intent to pull down Bawdy-houses; that *Basely* led them as their Captain, that *Messenger* had a green Apron upon a Staff, which he flourished as Colours, and then that *Appletree*, the Person now in Question, was amongst them both the Days, and was the first that struck at *Peverell* the Constable, and was amongst them at *Burlingham*'s House at *Saffron-hill*, and pulled part of that House down, and the next to it, and struck at one that admonished him to be quiet, so that here are several Acts of Force found to be actually committed by him in pursuance of their Design, and then there is no need to find him to be aiding and assisting, for that Clause we said was only necessary to be found where the Jury find a Person was there among them, and find no particular Act of Force done by him, but only his Presence, there it is necessary that they find he was present aiding and assisting; and for the same Reasons we held the Verdict to be full also against *Lattimer*, because it was first found that the Multitude was assembled as in the Indictment, on pretence of breaking Prisons and releasing Prisoners in general, which is agreed by all (except the Chief Baron) to be Treason, and then they find that *Lattimer* was amongst them, and active in the breaking open the Prison at *Clarkenwell*, (where Prisoners, some for Felony, and others were let loose) and that he was with the rest in the Prison after it was broken

open,

open, and so an Act fixed upon him: But although six of us were well satisfied in our Judgments as to them, yet when I waited on the King, I acquainted him that there was some difference in Opinion as to those two upon finding of the special Verdict; and although the greater Number of us were of Opinion, that the Verdict was well found as to those also, yet I intreated his Majesty to make use of that difference in Opinion to shew his Mercy towards them, the rather because we had agreed, that as to four of them the Verdict was clearly good as to proceed to Judgment against them, and that I hoped would be example enough to deter others from the like Practices; and besides it would appear an Instance of his Majesty's great Mercy, that he would not proceed to the last extremity against any, where there was not a full Concurrence of all his Judges, which his Majesty was pleased to take very graciously, and ordered me to proceed accordingly, and so they two were spared: But as to *Green* in the first special Verdict, and *Bedell* in the third special Verdict, we all agreed that the Verdict was not full enough as to them for us to judge it Treason in them, because the Verdict only finds that they were present, and finds no particular Act of Force committed by them, and doth not find that they were aiding and assisting to the rest, and it is possible one may be present amongst such a Rabble only out of curiosity to see, and whether they were aiding and assisting is matter of Fact which ought to be expresly found by the Jury, and not to be left to us upon any colourable Implication, and accordingly these two were discharged.

¹ Hawk. 55.

² St. Tr. 524.

² St. Tr. 59.

This Question was moved to me at the *Old Bailey*; A Man marrieth two Wives, one in *France* and another in *England*, whether he might be indicted and tryed for that Felony here in *England*; and I took this difference, that if his first Marriage was in *France*, and the second Marriage, which maketh the Felony, was in *England*, then I was of Opinion that he might be indicted and tryed here for it, and the Jury might on Evidence find his

A man marrieth two Wives, one in *France* and another in *England*, in what Case he may be tryed here.

² Hawk. 315.
¹ H.P.C. 693.

his first Marriage in *France*, being a mere transitory Act, and having nothing of Felony in it; and our *Juries* usually find such transitory Acts, though they are done in a Foreign Nation; but if the first Marriage was in *England*, and the second in *France*, then I was of Opinion he could not be tryed for it here, because the Act which made the Felony was done in another Kingdom, and Felonies done in another Kingdom, are not by the Common Law triable here in *England*. *Quære**:

*Diversity.
Vide Syderfin's Reports,
fo. 171.
1 Hawk. 171.*

By counterfeiting the Great Seal, what shall be Treason and what not, see *Co. pl. Cor. fol.* 15, 40. *Ass. pl.* 34, 42 *E.* 3. The Abbot of *Brewer*'s Case, who caused his Commoygn to raze the Name of one Manor in Letters Patent under the Great Seal, and to put in another Manor instead of it, and 2 *H.* 4. *fol.* 25. 37 *H.* 8. *Br. Title Treason.* But after all these Books was *George Leake*'s Case, a Clerk of the Chancery, who joined two clean Parchments fit for Letters Patents so close together with Mouth-glew, as they were taken for one, the uppermost being very thin, and did put one Label through both, then upon the uppermost he wrote a true Patent, and got the Great Seal put to the Label and the Seal were annexed to both the Parchments, the one written, the other a blank; then he cut off the glewed Skirts round about, and took off the uppermost thin Parchment in which the true Patent was writ from the Label which with the Great Seal did still hang to the blank Parchment, then he wrote another false Patent upon the blank Parchment and published it as a good Patent: And the Question was, whether this Offence was High Treason or not: And it was resolved by all the Judges of *England*, that this Offence was not High Treason, but it was a very great Misprision. *Vide Hale Pl. C.* 18.

*Counterfeiting the Great Seal.
1 Hawk. 61.*

*George Leak's Case concerning the abuse of the Great Seal.
Hill 4 Jacobi.
Coke 12 R. p. 16.
1 H.P.C. 182.*

* " Why not? For the Words of the Statute are, that the Par-
" ties so offending, shall receive such and the like Proceeding,
" Trial and Execution, in such County where such Person or Per-
" sons shall be apprehended, as if the Offence had been commit-
" ted in such County where such Persons shall be taken or appre-
" hended." 1 Hawk 175, and Notis ibid.

A Per-

A Person hireth Lodgings in another Man's House, with Hangings, Bedding, and other Furniture in those Lodging for a Month, and during that Time, conveyeth away the Goods in the Lodging which he had hired with the Lodging, and the Party runeth away at the same Time, and is after taken and indicted for this as for Felony, and whether this be Felony or not is the Question. *This is not found in the original Manuscript, but may be fit to be reported, because said to come from Mr. Serjeant Kelyng, Son to the Chief Justice. 1 Hawk. 137. and Not. ibi.*

This Case is in this Book, and came before my Lord *Bridgman*, then Chief Justice of the Common Pleas, myself then Judge of the King's Bench, and my Brother *Wylde*, then Recorder of *London*, at a Sessions in the *Old Bailey*, and then we all were of Opinion that this was no Felony, because the Party had a special Property in the Goods by his Contract, and so there could be no Trespass, and that there could be no Felony where there was no Trespass, as was resolved in *Holmes*'s Case, who set Fire to his own House, which was quenched before it went any further, and accordingly the Prisoner was by us then discharged. *Vide Ante 24. Raven's Case. 1 Jon 351. Cro.Car. 376, 7. Ante 29. Sed vide Fost. 116.*

But upon more serious Thoughts I take it to be a Case worthy of great Consideration, because I think the Case in the 13 *Ed.* 4. *fo.* 9. which was by the King and his Council referred to all the Judges in the *Chequer-Chamber*, and by them resolved to be Felony, is a stronger Case than the Case now put.

There the Case was, one bargained with another to carry some Packs of Goods for him to *Southampton*, and delivered the Goods to the Carrier, and he taketh them and carries them to another Place, and there opens the Packs, and takes the Goods, and disposes of them to his own Use, and the Question was, whether that was Felony

Felony or not; and though it was objected that the Goods were bailed to the Carrier, and therefore there could be no Felony, that was agreed generally to be good Law. And it was also objected that an Indictment against one that he *felonice asportavit*, such Goods is not good, but it must be *felonice cepi & asportavit*, and in that Case the taking was lawful; yet it was resolved that it was Felony, because his subsequent Act of carrying the Goods to another Place, and there opening of them, and disposing of them to his own Use, declareth that his Intent originally was not to take the Goods upon the Agreement and Contract of the Party, but only with a Design of stealing them. Now methinks the Case in Question is much stronger: For in that, the Party himself cometh to hire the Lodgings and Goods, and when he after taketh them away, this declareth that his original Intent was only by the hiring of them to give himself the Opportunity to steal them, and so his first hiring them is, *in fraudem Legis*, and of that he shall take no Advantage, *Co. Pl. Cor.* 64. Some under pretence of a Robbery raise a Hue and Cry, and call a Constable to search a House in the Night Time, and the Constable coming, the Owner of the House, opens the Door, and then those Persons bind the Constable, and those in the House, and Rob them, this is Burglary; because they procured the Door to be opened to them in the Night by Fraud: So in this Case, the Party hiring the House by Fraud, only to have an Opportunity to steal the Goods, shall not take Benefit of the Fraud. And Mr. *Lee* told me, that it had been resolved, that, *if one come into* Smithfield *on pretence to buy a Horse, and cheapen one, and the Owner giveth him leave to take the Horse and ride him to try his paces, and then he taketh the Horse and rideth quite away with him, this is Felony*. And if one deliver Goods to a Porter in *London* to carry to a certain Place, and he taketh them and carrieth them away to another Place, and there openeth and disposeth of them, this is Felony; which last Case seemeth to be warranted by the Case before cited out of 13 *E.* 4. *Note*, That the breaking open the Packs and

1 H P.C. 552.
1 Hawk. 161.

and difpofing of the Goods is neceffary to fhew the Intent of ftealing.

But I marvel at the Cafe put, 13 *E.* 4. 9. That if a Carrier have a Tun of Wine delivered to him to carry to fuch a Place, and he never carry it but fell it, all this is no Felony; but if he draw part of it out above the Value of Twelve-pence, this is Felony; I do not fee why the difpofing of the Whole fhould not be Felony alfo.

But the Cafe there put is, a Carrier does carry the Goods to the Place appointed, and after takes them away and difpofeth of them, that is Felony, becaufe the Bargain for his bringing them was determined when he brought them to that Place appointed, and the Poffeffion then is in the firft Owner.

A Man having a Dwelling-houfe lets a Cellar, to which the Paffage is out of a Street and a Chamber, to *J. S.* and lieth in the Chamber, and the Cellar is broken open in the Night. If this be Burglary? I thought not, and took a difference betwixt an Inmate and a divided Houfe, which is, where there are feveral Doors, and one Dwelling actually divided and feparated from the other, there it is Burglary, and fhall be laid for breaking the Dwelling-houfe of him who hired the divided Part. But as to an Inmate who goeth in at the fame Door, he is in the Nature of a Lodger, and if his Chamber be broken open, I thought it Burglary. But you muft lay the Indictment for breaking the Dwelling-houfe of him that let it, and not of the Inmate, becaufe I thought it was but one Dwelling-houfe, in cafe there be twenty Inmates: And though there be a private Contract between the Parties, that hath not fevered the Dwelling-houfe, fo as to make them feveral Dwelling-houfes. For then, what need that difference of Inmates and divided Houfes? For

1 Hawk. 164. Contra. But with a Quære in the Margin.

1 Hawk. 161. 1 H.P.C. 356. Contra. 1 Hawk. 163. Cowper 2.

if an Inmate hath a divided Dwelling-house, he differs nothing from the other. But Mr. *Lee* desired that it might be advised of, because he saith their use hath been otherwise, and he said that else, if the Rooms of the Inmate where he lieth were broken open in the Night Time, there would be no Burglary, because he said the Contract had severed them from the Dwelling-house of him who let them. But in that I differed; for I think that where there is but one out Door, at which the Owner and Inmate enter, this remaineth to be all the Dwelling-house of the Owner; and though the Inmate hath an Interest against the Owner that will not serve to make it the Dwelling-house of the Inmate. But the Indictment must be for Burglary, in breaking the Dwelling-house of the Owner, and stealing the Goods of the Inmate. (*Quære.*)

1 H. P. C. Contra 556.
1 H.P.C. 537.

But for the first Question, where a Cellar which hath its going into it only out of the Street is let to a stranger; if this Cellar is broken open, I conceive it no Burglary, for it is separated by the Contract, and actually severed from the House by excluding all Communication with the House, no passing being betwixt the House and the Cellar. So it hath been resolved, if a Man let a Shop only, and sever it from his House for Years, &c. and the Party who hath the Shop doth not lodge in it, and this be broke open in the Night, this is no Burglary. And how to make such a Cellar and a Chamber in the Dwelling-house, which are let to an Inmate to be the Inmate's Dwelling-house, I do not well understand: Then Mr. *Lee* said it might be of ill Consequence; for now since the late Fire, every House hath many Inmates, where Inmates Lodge. And suppose he who hath the Dwelling-house (and lets the several Rooms to those Inmates) should in the Night break open their Rooms and steal their Goods, it would be hard if it should not be Burglary. To that I say it is Felony in the Owner of the House, if he steal their Goods; but to make it Burglary to break his own House, in case the Law be as I suppose, that cannot be. And I suppose letting of Lodgings to several Persons, doth not make several Houses if they all go in at the Door of him who lets the Lodgings, and so are but Inmates.

1 Hawk. 163 contra.

But

But otherwife it is, if a Man fever fome Rooms from his Houfe, and make another Door to thofe Rooms, and fo divide the Houfe, that divided Part is the Manfion-houfe of him who hires it; and fhall be laid fo, for breaking the Dwelling-houfe of him who hired that Part *.

* See vide 1 Hawk. 163, 164. Sect. 14, 15, and Note to this laft Section, where this Doctrine is controverted.

TERM.

TERM. MICH.

15 CAR. II. In B. R.

---

1 Sid. 159.
1 Keb. 584,
649, 659, 723.
S. C.

Sir Charles Stanley's Case.

This is another Manuscript of the Lord Chief Justice Kelyng.
1 Hawk. 121, 9.

SIR *Charles Stanley* and one *Andrews*, were tryed upon an Indictment of Murder. The Case was, Sir *Charles Stanley* was arrested by a Bailiff, and endeavoured a Rescue, and shot off a Pistol at the Bailiff, and then the Bailiff closed with him and cast him down, and after some of his Servants and others who came to aid him, killed a Servant of the Bailiff's who came in aid of the Bailiff: And it was resolved by all the Court, *Hide*, Chief Justice

Justice, *Twisden*, *Windham*, and *Kelyng*, that if the Party who is arrested doth any Act of Violence to endeavour a Rescue, and then after one of his Party killed the Bailiff, or any that cometh in his aid, this is Murder in the Party arrested: For when several Men join in an unlawful Act they are all guilty of whatever happens upon it; and in the Lord *Dacre's* Case which is mentioned, 34 *H.* 8. *Brooke Sect.* 237*. The Lord *Dacres* and *Mansell*, and others in his Company came unlawfully to hunt in a Forest, and being resisted, one of the Company when the Lord *Dacres* was a great Way off, and not present, killed a Man: Judged Murder in him and all the Rest, and the Lord *Dacres* was hanged. But it was agreed, that if the Party who is arrested yields himself, and makes no Resistance, but others endeavour to rescue him, and he doth not act to declare his joining with them, if those who come to rescue him kill any of the Bailiffs, this is Murder in them, but not in the Party arrested. But in this Case Sir *Charles Stanley* by shooting his Pistol, had joined in resisting the Authority of Law, and therefore a Man being slain in this Act, it is Murder in him. And as for *Andrews*, there was no Evidence, but out of his own Mouth; some discourse as if he had shot over Sir *Charles Stanley* in aid of him when he was down, but the Evidence to that was slight. But it was agreed by us all, that if a Man be arrested, and while they are fighting, one who knows nothing of the Arrest coming by the Way, goeth in aid of the Person who is arrested, and draws his Sword, &c. here if any of the Bailiffs be killed, that Person who joined in aid against them, though he did not know of the Arrest, yet is guilty of Murder. For a Man must take heed how he joineth in any unlawful Act as fighting is, for if he doth, he is guilty of all that follows. And it being Murder to kill those who come to execute the Law; every one who joins in that Act is guilty of Murder, and his Ignorance will not excuse him, where the Fact is made Murder by the Law without any Malice precedent, as in the Case of killing

Moore 86.
1 H.P.C. 439, 465.
Crompt. 25.
Dalt. J. Cap. 93. p. 241.
n. ed. Cap. 145. p. 472.

---

* The above Blank is in the principal Case in the Edition of this Work, published by Sir *John Holt*; but the Case there cited is to be found in Moore 80, and it is there said to be in *Easter*, 10 *Eliz.* though *Brooke* Tit. Corone 171, (and not 237,) as above cited. It is said to be as in the Text, and *Crompton*, who cites for this Case *Stowe's* Annals, fo. 582, also fixes it in 34 H. 8.

killing a Bailiff. But if two Men go upon Malice prepenſed to fight a Duel, and while they are fighting, a Man who is acquainted with one of them joineth and taketh his Part and killeth the other, this is Murder in the Party who came with Malice prepenſed to fight; but it is but Manſlaughter in him who came to his aid, becauſe in him there was no Malice, but as to him it was a ſudden Thing. And here the Law doth not imply Malice, as it doth in every one who refiſteth the Execution of Juſtice.

1 H.P.C. 665.

MICHAELMAS

TERM. MICH.

8. WILL. 3.

Lisle's Case, in *Banco Regis*.

AT the *Assizes* and *Gaol Delivery* held for the County of *Cumberland*, at *Carlisle*, 15 *Aug.* last, before Sir *Edward Ward* Lord Chief Baron, and Justice *Turton*, *Thomas Lisle* Gent. was indicted for the Murder of *Richard Armstrong*, upon which he was arraigned, tried, and convicted of Manslaughter only. Immediately after, *John Armstrong*, brother of *Richard*, put into the Court a Bill of Appeal for Murder, and did then pray his Council, that the Appeal should be received and filed, and that *Lisle* should be immediately arraigned thereupon. Whereupon, and before the Appeal was arraigned, *Lisle* did demand the Benefit of his Clergy; and then the Bill of Appeal by the Council of *Armstrong* was read in open Court, and *Lisle* did appear thereunto, and prayed to be bailed, but refused to plead; upon which he was remanded to the Gaol *quousque*, *&c.* All which Proceeding was entered upon the Record of the Indictment of Murder, with the Conviction of Manslaughter, and returned upon a *Certiorari* into this Court, and thereupon the Appeal of Murder was also returned; but upon the Record of that, no Mention was made of any Proceeding. *Lisle* was also brought to the Bar upon an *Habeas Corpus* directed to the Sheriff of *Cumberland*, and was committed to the *Marshalsea*,

Trem. 20.
Skinner 670.
Carthew 394.
Comb 410.
Salk. 60.
12 Mod. 108,
109, 157.
Holt 53. S. C.

shulsea, (though he prayed to be bailed;) but the Court did not think fit to bail him for the Present; for it being the latter-end of the Term, did adjourn the Confideration of it to the next Term; at which Time *Lifle* being brought to the Bar by Rule, the Court was of Opinion that he might be bailed. The Queftion was, whether one convicted of Manflaughter might be bailed before he had his Clergy? The Cafe of *Dyer* 297 & 42 *. is, that he cannot be bailed; which may be admitted to be Law, for though Juftices of *Oyer* and *Terminar* and *Gaol Delivery*, might not bail in fuch a Cafe, yet the *King's Bench* is not reftrained from bailing by the Statute of 1 *W. c.* 5. 2 *Inft.* 885. but hath a Liberty of bailing by the Common Law, if the Perfon be not attainted. And fo was it done in this Court, 10 *Jac. Coke's Entries* 355 †. upon the like Conviction of Manflaughter, upon a Trial at the Bar: The Court, without calling the Party to Judgment, took Time to advife until the next Term, and bailed the Prifoner then to appear. Afterwards at another Day, it was queftioned, whether the Court fhould call *Lifle* to know what he could fay why Judgment fhould not be given againft him, and if he fhould demand the Benefit of his Clergy, allow it to him? And after Argument at the Bar it was refolved, that forafmuch as there was a *Record of Conviction returned to the* King's Bench, *the Court ought to proceed to Judgment thereupon, though there was an Appeal returned to be commenced.*

2 Hawk. 153.
S r. 911.
Rex v Dalton 1242.
Rex v. Magrath.

For thefe Reafons:

1. Though the Appeal was not totally difcontinued, but had an Exiftence, yet it was without Day; for being commenced at the *Gaol Delivery*, it had no continuance upon it, nor indeed could it have any, for no continuance can be taken from one Seffion of *Gaol Delivery* to another, but from one Day to another it may be, if that Seffion be adjourned, which doth not appear in this Cafe; but all Proceedings upon Indictments and Appeals commenced

2 Hawk. 234.
Note to Sect 10.
Carth. 394, 395.
Skinner 670.
Bac. Abr. 126.

---

* This ought to be, as I believe, Dyer 179. Pl. 42.
† Tit *Indictment*, Pl. 6.

at one *Gaol Delivery*, unlefs Convictions thereupon, are determined by that Seffion, fo that this Appellant and Appellee have no Day in any Court; and the Appeal being removed into the *King's Bench*, the Parties having no Day in the Court, the only means to retrieve it, is, for the Appellant to come into Court, and pray that the Appellee being *in cuftodia Marr'* may be arraigned; and if he was not in the Marfhal's Cuftody, take Procefs againft him, 9 *H.* 4. 2. *St. P. C.* 651*. which may be done at any Time. But if the Appellee be defirous to be difcharged of the Appeal, then he ought to fue a *Scire facias* againft the Appellant, and if he doth not appear nonfuit him, *St. P. C.* 70. *a. b.* From hence it is to be concluded, that fince the Appeal is without Day, and cannot be proceeded upon unlefs revived in the Manner before mentioned, there is no Reafon for the Court to take any Notice of it, but to proceed upon the Conviction had upon the Indictment, as if no Appeal had been commenced.

2. The Court, as the Matter ftands upon this Record, ought to proceed upon the Conviction; for it appears that not only the Indictment was preferred, but even the Trial and Conviction of Manflaughter was before the Appeal commenced; and therefore by the exprefs Words of 3 *H.* 7. *That in Cafe of Murder, the Murderers fhall at any Time be arraigned and determined at the King's Suit, within the Year, without tarrying for an Appeal* †. Now the Indictment being proceeded upon, and the Party tried before the Appeal commenced, the Court of *Gaol Delivery* ought to determine it; for though the Appeal interpofes after Conviction, and before the Convict upon the Indictment is called to Judgment, yet the Judgment upon it hath relation to the Conviction, and on the giving of it no Notice is to be taken of the Appeal, nor is any Entry to be on Record, to hinder the Court from giving Judgment. And if the Trial was lawful, the Judgment thereupon muft be as lawful, for otherwife it would be in the Power of a Perfon by putting in an Appeal to render the Verdict ineffectual, which is contrary to the Words and Intent of the Statute; for fuppofe

2 Hawk. 355.

* St. Pl. Cor. 165—as I believe.
† The contrary of this Doctrine feem to be holden by Coke. 3 Inft. 131.

the

the Conviction had been for Murder, the Indictment being well commenced and proceeded upon, the subsequent Appeal cannot obstruct Judgment, but the Court ought to condemn the Prisoner, otherwise the Statute of 3 *H.* 7. is not observed, which requires not only a Proceeding on the Indictment, but a Determination: And the Statute would be as little observed if Judgment should be respited upon the Conviction of Manslaughter as upon a Conviction of Murder.

2 Hawk. 535.

3. By the Common Law no Conviction or Acquittal could be avoided by an Appeal interposing before Judgment: but though Judgment was respited, the Defendant in the Appeal might plead the Acquittal or Conviction had in Bar to the Appeal, *St. P. C.* 106. 16 *E.* 4.

3 Inst. 131. S. C.

11. 45 *E.* 3, 25. 4 *Rep.* 45. *Wrote* and *Wigges;* against which there are but two Cases, *viz.* 17 *Ass. p.* 1. which are contradicted by the Opinion and Observation of *B. tit. Appeal* 55. that declares the Common Law to be contrary until 3 *H.* 7. The other is *Dyer* 296. *p.* 20. which

Stanley's Case.

is so very strange, that it cannot amount to the least Authority. That Case was, *viz.* One indicted of Murder was convicted at the Gaol Delivery of *Newgate*, and before Judgment given the Wife brought an Appeal; to which the Defendant pleaded, that she had taken another Husband in a Foreign Country. The Matter resting about a Year, the Indictment was removed in *B. R.* and the Party convicted called to Judgment upon the Indictment, and he pleaded the Appeal depending; to which *Nul tiel Record* was pleaded; but afterwards the Plaintiff in the Appeal was non-suited, and then Judgment of Death was given against the Defendant. *Observe,* That Case is left with a *Quære,* and so no judicial Determination as to this Point, saving that the Man was hanged.

1. The Court gave no Opinion concerning the sufficiency of the Plea.

2. It doth not appear how the Plaintiff became Non-suit.

For

For there was not any Opportunity for it, therefore it was irregular; for the Plea was difcontinued by the *Certiorari;* for all Removals of Caufes upon *Certiorari*'s determine the Plea; therefore that Cafe is no Authority, but only an Hiftory of what was done; for the Man was well condemned and executed upon the Conviction, and thofe Scruples then made were very unneceffary.

For which Reafons the Court did arraign *Lifle* upon the Conviction of Manflaughter, and he demanded his Clergy; which being allowed to him, he read as a Clerk, and was burnt in the Hand.

Armftrong verfus *Lifle*.

Mich. 8 *W.* 3. *Rot.* 565.

IN the Appeal of Murder before mentioned, the Defendant fued out a *Scire facias* againft the Plaintiff to profecute his Appeal, returnable *Quinden' Pafch'*; at which Day the Plaintiff appeared, and by his Council at Bar did arraign the Appeal. It being prayed that the Defendant might anfwer thereunto, the Defendant pleaded the Indictment, and Conviction of Manflaughter at the Affizes, which was removed into the *King's Bench*; and that no Judgment was thereupon given; and that at the Time of the Conviction he was, and yet is a Clerk; and then prayed his Clergy, and offered to read as a Clerk if the Court would have admitted him thereunto; and that afterwards, on *Monday poft Craftin' Pur' Beatæ Mariæ Virginis* laft, being demanded by the Court why Judgment fhould not be given againft him, he demanded the Benefit of Clergy; which being allowed to him, he read as a Clerk, and was burned in the Hand *prout per Recordum*, &c. with the ufual Averments. And as to the Felony and Murder pleaded *Not Guilty*. To which Plea the

2 H.P.C. 390.
2 Hawk. 535.

Plaintiff

Plaintiff made a frivolous Replication, and the Defendant thereunto demurred.

2 Hawk. 534.   The Question was, whether this Plea was a good Bar to the Appeal? And it was resolved by the whole Court, that the Defendant being convicted of Manslaughter, and allowed the Benefit of Clergy, and reading as a Clerk, did bar the Apellant of his Appeal of Murder. And though the Reasons given in the former Case may be sufficient to justify this Resolution; yet many Things may be fit to be added for further Explication of this Matter, which hath for a long Time been in much obscurity, and laboured under very great variety of Opinion.

2 Hawk. 535.   1. The Conviction or Acquittal upon an Indictment of Murder or Manslaughter was at Common Law, a good Plea in Bar to the Appeal. For the Proceeding upon the Indictment may be Legal, though the Appeal was then pending; and if the Party convicted should have had Judgment of Death given against him if he was no Clerk, there is the same Reason he should have the Benefit of the Conviction and Clergy if he were a Clerk. The like if he be acquitted; for if convicted he should suffer Death, therefore if acquitted he should be discharged.

2 Hawk. 535.   To the Authorities before cited, these may be added, *F. N. B.* 115. *h.* where an Appeal of Murder was depending, if within the Year and the Day, the Justices of Gaol Delivery did proceed to try the Appellee upon an Indictment of Murder, and he was acquitted, he might have a Writ of Conspiracy, though he was not tried upon the Appeal; which could not have been maintained unless the Acquittal upon the Indictment had been a perfect and absolute Discharge of the Offence, 21 *H.* 6. 28. *Fitz.* tit *Conspiracy* 6. 7. *H.* 4. 35. *Hale* 244. That an Acquittal upon an Indictment is a good Bar to an Appeal of Murder. The reason whereof is more strong in the Case of an Appeal of Death than in any other Appeal, *to wit*, of *Robbery* or *Larceny*, (in which an Acquittal upon an Indictment would be, and is to this Day, a good

good Bar) *St. Pl. Cor.* 106. For the Appellant seeks only Revenge for the Death of his Anceftor, without regard to the Publick: But in an Appeal of *Robbery* or *Larceny*, he is to have Reftitution: but if a Perfon be murdered, the King profecutes to have an Example of Juftice made for the Safety of all his People; befides, the King is more concerned in Intereft, being to have the Forfeiture of all the Goods and Chattels of the Offender, and the Year, Day, and Wafte of his Lands.

And though the Profecution at the King's Suit was frequently delayed for the Benefit of the Parties Appeal, yet that was not *ex provifione Legis*, but merely by the Difcretion of the Judges, for the more effectual Profecution of the Offender, by encouraging the Perfons who where moft concerned, and therefore were thought to be moft zealous therein. This appears by *St. Pl. Cor.* 107. *Fitz. tit. Coron.* 44. 22 *E.* 4. when the Juftices did agree, that that courfe of delaying to proceed on the Indictment within the Year fhould be obferved, for the fake of the Parties Appeal, which was frequently practifed before, but not fo firmy eftablifhed until then. *Hale Pl. Cor. con.* fo 40 *Aff. p.* 40. But the Mifchief thereof being in fome few Years perceived, occafioned the making the Statute of 3 *H.* 7. which abolifhed that Liberty which the Judges took, and obliged them to proceed upon the Indictment at any Time within the Year, and upon no Account to tarry for the Appeal; and to encourage that Proceeding, faves the Benefit of the Appeal, notwithftanding the Attainder or Acquittal, except when Clergy was had; for that Exception is to the Purview of the Statute, and fhews what the Law was before, *viz. That when Clergy was had upon a Conviction or Attainder of Murder upon the Indictment, it was a good Bar of the Appeal before the Statute.*

2 Hawk. 530.
2 Hawk. 535.

Sum. 245.
2 Hale P. C. 251.

It is moft true, that if an Appeal was frefhly brought, and pending before the fame Juftices before whom the Appellee was indicted, the Court ought to proceed rather upon the Appeal than the Indictment, becaufe of the

2 Hawk. 530.
2 Hawk. 535.

Intereft

Intereſt of the Appellant, who in Caſe of Robbery ought to have Reſtitution, which upon an Indictment before 21 *H.* 8. he could not have; and in an Appeal of Death the Wife or heir might have Execution upon the Judgment (notwithſtanding any Pardon) in Revenge of the Injury done to her or him: And the preferring the Appeal then pending, to the Indictment, was no hurt to the Publick Juſtice of the Kingdom; for if the Appellant was nonſuited, or did releaſe either before or after Attainder, the Proſecution was devolved to the King, who might cauſe proceeding to be upon the Appeal, and Execution to be had upon the Indictment. But at the Common Law, if there was a default of freſh Suit, the Appeal was loſt, if the Defendant did plead it in Abatement. *Vide Stat. Glouc. cap.* 9. *Bract. lib* 3. 139*. 2 *Inſt.* 319. *Qui appellare voluerit, debet ille cui injuratum fuerit, tam cito quam poterit, Huteſium levare, &c.* Therefore by ſuch a neglect of freſh Suit, the Proſecution belonged to the King to proceed by way of Indictment. But in that Caſe the Appellee, upon an appeal commenced againſt him, could not take advantage of the want of freſh Suit, unleſs he had pleaded it   And in an Appeal of Robbery or Larceny, though the Defendant did not plead in Abatement the want of freſh Suit, but was thereupon convicted, yet the Appellant could not have Reſtitution unleſs the Jury did find freſh Suit.

2 Hawk. 530, 535.

But great Queſtion hath been made, of what ſhould be accounted a freſh Suit? *Vide St. Pl. Cor.* 165, 166. where, upon Conſideration of all the Books, it is ſettled, *that it is not capable of any certain Definition, but muſt be determined by the Diſcretion of the Juſtices.* Now if the Party robbed, be not as ready to proſecute his Appeal, before the Juſtices of Gaol Delivery, as the King's Officers are to proſecute an Indictment, and the Offender be in Gaol; or if the Party ſhall chuſe rather to Proſecute upon the Indictment; this is a neglect of the Appeal, and a default of freſh Suit, ſo far as to veſt the Proſecution in the King; for though it is very reaſonable to prefer

* Britton fol. 43. accord.

fer the Appeal to the Indictment, yet there can be no Reason to defer the King's Prosecution by any affected delay in the Party that should bring his Appeal. Therefore, if at any Time the Court did proceed upon an Indictment, when an Appeal was depending; it must be presumed, that the Person injured was negligent or remiss in the Prosecution of the Appeal, or that the Appeal was convenously brought to obstruct the King's Prosecution, which is the same in Judgment of Law, as if none was brought at all, or that the Party did choose to proceed upon the Indictment rather than the Appeal. And therefore at the Common Law in case of Death, and then, and now, in that of all other Felony, if one were tried and acquitted upon an Indictment, if the Person injured did bring his Appeal, and the Defendant did plead his acquittal, the Appellant could not reply that he brought his Appeal by fresh Suit; for that would be to arraign the Justice of the Court in a matter that is left to be tried by Examination; and to be determined by the Justices, for the Appellant might bring his Appeal convenously, or if really, chose rather to proceed upon the Indictment.

Obj. But there is an Objection that seems plausible, 2 Hawk. 530, which is, that before the Statute of 3 *Hen.* 7. the Court 335. was obliged by Law, not to proceed upon the Indictment of Murder within the Year and a Day; for though at Common Law, the Appellant was to make fresh Suit; yet the Statute of *Glouc. chap.* 9. hath given a Year and a Day to the Appellant to bring his Appeal, which is instead of fresh Suit: And therefore where there was fresh Suit, the Court ought rather to proceed upon the Appeal, than upon the Indictment. And since the Party hath a Year and a Day to bring his Appeal, there can be no default imputed to him until that Time be expired.

Resp. To this I answer. First, that the King, as to 2 Hawk. 530, his Prosecution is not obliged by any Words in the Sta- 555. tute, but only the Defendant, if the Appeal be brought within the Year, is disabled to plead in Abatement thereof
the

the want of fresh Suit. For the Statute was made for the advancement of Justice; but if there should be such a Consequence deduced from it, that the Defendant could not be tried upon the Indictment within the Year, it would tend much to the delay of Justice.

Resp. Secondly, it appears, not only by all the Books before mentioned, that the not proceeding upon the Indictment was only an Agreement among the Judges themselves; but the recital of the Statute of 3 *H.* 7. doth not mention that, that delay was by Law; but only that it was used to tarry.

<small>2 Hawk. 530, 535.</small>

Resp. 3. Thirdly, That Agreement of the Judges plainly shews, that if the Defendant had been tried and acquitted or convicted, that would have been a good Bar to the Appeal, otherwise that delay would have been to no Purpose.

<small>2 Hawk. 530, 535. 2 Hawk. 534.</small>

Resp. 4. Fourthly, the Defendant in the Appeal could not hinder his being tried upon the Indictment, for he could not plead the Appeal depending, either in Bar, or in delay of the Trial, 43 *E.* 3. 25. *a.* 31 *H.* 6. 11. Now, if he was tried and acquitted upon the Indictment, and yet should be liable to the Party's Appeal, his Life must be twice in Jeopardy; so that though the Judges did do an Injury to the Appellant in trying the Prisoner upon the Indictment, either within the Year, or pending the Appeal, (which is not to be supposed) yet that ought not to affect the Appellee, who could not prevent his being tried.

<small>2 Hawk. 530, 35.</small>

It is in the next Place to be considered, whether the Court can delay the allowing of Clergy, to a Prisoner convicted of a Crime within the Benefit of it. And if the Court should respite the Allowance of Clergy, what the Consequence would be.

The Court ought not to delay the Party having the Benefit of his Clergy; for it is his Right, if he be capable of it [*]. *Hob.* 289. *Searle* against *Williams.* First, it may

---

[*] Though the Judges made it a Rule not to admit any one to Clergy, until after he had pleaded; yet I find it no where holden that a Man could not legally demand it until called to Judgment: Nor doth the Opinion to the Contrary, in the principal Case, grounded on the Authority in Hobart, seem to be at all made out by that Case. 2 Hawk. 536.

Armstrong versus Lisle.

not be improper to enquire how his Right of having Clergy did commence. Secondly, how Laymen came to be entitled to it. This Right began by an Encroachment of the Pope upon the Temporal Power, in the Behalf of the Clergy; whom the Pope by his Ecclesiastical Constitutions did as much as in him lay, exempt from the Jurisdiction of Lay Judges. Therefore, though the whole Body of the Clergy stood upon it, as appears by St. *Ar' Cler' C.* 15. that *Clericus coram Seculari Judice judicari non debet* in case of Life or Member; yet the Temporal Courts did not wholly yield to this Imposition, but only in Part, and qualified it in a great Measure. 2 Hawk. 474. 2 In.st. 633.

1. They would indict Clerks for Felonies and Crimes, as well as others, and proceed thereon, until the Ordinary did demand them. And if the Ordinary would not demand them, antiently, the King's Courts took no Notice of them; but would proceed to Conviction, Attainder and Execution. And if the Ordinary did claim Clerks before Conviction, then an Inquisition was taken, whether the Party was Guilty or not, *ut sciatur qualis Ordinario deliberatur*, and if acquitted, discharged; but if found Guilty, then delivered to the Ordinary, who was to proceed to Purgation. This Privilege so restrained and ordered, was confirmed and established by the Statute of *W.* 1. *cap.* 2. and thereby became an undoubted right to all Clerks; which was confirmed and allowed by divers Acts of Parliament since. But then the Ordinary was to proceed to deprive the Clerk of his Character, if he could not purge, whereby he became a meer Layman: For though at first the Clergy never intended that any should have that Privivilege, but those who were in Holy Orders; yet afterwards they extended it to those who were not strictly in Orders, but were Assistants to them in doing Divine Offices. See *Linwood* 92. That they should have the Privilege of Clergy, who had but *primam tonsuram*, which for the Purpose was the Clerk that sung or set the *Psalm*, who was comprehended under the Word *Clericus*, *Linwood* 17. So was the Door-keeper of the 2 Hawk. 504.

Church or Chapel, the Reader, Exorcist, Sub-Deacon, which becaufe the Temporal Courts did not readily allow, occafioned the Complaint of the Clergy, as appears by the Statute in 25 *E*. 3. *cap*. 4. That *Clerks Seculars, &c.* had been drawn and hanged, by the award of fecular Judges; in prejudice of the Franchizes, and in Oppofition to the Jurifdiction of Holy Church. Therefore it was granted by the King, that all manner of Clerks, as well fecular as Religious, which fhould be convicted before fecular Juftices, fhould have that Privilege; which Word Clerk in that Statute hath reference to the Canon Law, and being made to eftablifh a Privilege claimed thereby was expounded by it, which included all that were of thofe inferior Orders. And from thence it is to be obferved, Occafion was taken in after-times to alter the Method of allowing Clergy, for at the Common Law, if the Party had not demanded his Clergy before Conviction, he loft it, *St. P. C.* 151. *Prifot* Chief Juftice of the *Common*

a Hawk. 504. *Pleas* in the Time of *H.* 6. made an Alteration, and would direct the Party indicted or appealed to anfwer to the Felony, and after Conviction upon his own Demand allow him his Clergy, which Courfe has been ever fince obferved, being grounded upon the faid Statute of 25 *E.* 3. *cap*. 4. that allows it to Clerks after Conviction.

2 Hawk. 474. Now the next enquiry will be how mere Laymen, who had no Relation to any Ecclefiaftical Employment came to enjoy this Privilege. It is to be known that in thofe Days few were bred to Literature, but thofe who were actually in Orders, or educated for that Purpofe. And therefore the way of Trial whether one was a Clerk or not was by reading, of which the Court was Judge, and not the Ordinary; for if he could not read, the Court would not deliver him as a Clerk, though the Ordinary did claim him. And if he did read, he fhould be allowed as a Clerk, though the Ordinary refufed him. See *St. Pl. C.* 131, 132. where the Books are quoted, the variety of Opinions confidered, and the Law fettled. And reading

being

being the Way of Trial, whether a Man were a Clerk or not, without further Examination into any other Qualification, all Persons that so approved themselves by reading were allowed to be Clerks, which is an equitable Conſtruction of thoſe Statutes, that eſtabliſhed and extended that Privilege, becauſe they were tried and found by their reading to be Clerks.

And further, the allowing Clergy to Lay-men that 2 Hawk. 474. could read, ſeemed very much in Favour of the Clergy, in preſerving its Succeſſion, by exempting ſuch who were capable of receiving any Orders, when there was occaſion for their Service: For though Men were never ſo well qualified for being Clergymen; yet by the Canon Law, which is ſtill in Force, they were not to receive any Orders, until a Place was provided for them; which favourable Conſtruction of the Statutes in not confining the Benefit of Clergy to thoſe who were actually in Orders, but who were capable of them, received conſtant Approbation and Allowance. See 4 *Hen.* 7. *cap.* 13. that enacts, that every Perſon not being within Holy Orders, that once had the Benefit of his Clergy, ſhould not be admitted to it any other Time. And the like Act was made 4 *Hen.* 8. which for Murders, Robberies &c. excludes all Perſons from the Benefit of his Clergy, (Clerks in Holy Orders excepted;) which gave much Offence to the Clergy, becauſe the Conſtruction of the Words Holy Orders, was confined to the greateſt Orders, as Deacon and Preſbiter, excluding not ony Lay-men, but all the inferior Orders, whoſe Orders are not accounted ſacred. See *Linwood* 92. for they had only *primam Tonſuram*, which cauſed the Abbot of *Winchomb* in his Sermon at *Paul's Croſs* to inveigh againſt that Act; and to avoid the Force of it againſt thoſe of the inferior Orders, the Clergy inſiſted, that *tam minores quam majores Ordines fuere ſacri.* See *Keil* 180. the whole Debate of that Matter *.

That Lay-men, that could read, ever had the Privilege of Clergy ſince 25 *E.* 3. doth appear without contradic-

* Pl. 5.

tion

tion by our Books, which allowance never was condemned in Parliament, or complained of as a Grievance; but rather approved of. And the Statute of 18 *Eliz.* being made, extends to all Perfons, that at that Time were admitted to the Ordinary; whereby every Perfon, as well Lay, as Spiritual, hath a right to the Benefit of that Statute for the firſt Offence, in the fame Degree as Clergymen in the greateſt Orders had before. The Statute enacts that:

2 Hawk. 510.

1. One that ſhall be admitted to the Benefit of his Clergy, (which is, every one that demands it and Reads) ſhall not be delivered to the Ordinary: But after reading, and burning in the Hand ſhall be delivered; which amounts to, and hath the fame effect as a Purgation before. *Vide* 5 *Rep.* 115: *Foxley's Cafe.*

2 Hawk. 508.

2. If the Offence be heynous, the Court in Difcretion may inflict any other Punifhment, not exceeding a Year's Imprifonment; whereby there is no room left for the Court to exclude him from the Benefit of his Clergy, upon which his Difcharge depends. And if it be fo heynous, the Court ought to proceed regularly and give him that additional Punifhment, that the Law doth direct after Clergy had. So that the Court is bound up to that Manner of Proceeding, which the Statute had prefcribed; but to remand to Gaol without doing either, is without any Warrant, Rule or Method in Law, and contrary not only to 18 *Eliz.* and 3 *Hen.* 7. but to the 25 *Ed.* 3. In the recital whereof, complaint was made that Clerks being attainted, were remanded to Gaol upon a Suggeſtion that other Matters were againſt them; yet the Law was, that thoſe Clerks ſhould not be remanded to Gaol, but prefently arraigned of all againſt them, otherwife immediately delivered to the Ordinary, fo that he ought not to be kept longer than the fame Seffion or Gaol Delivery, though he was indicted for other Crimes. *Vide St. Pl. C.* 152.

1. It

Armstrong versus Lisle.

It is not enough to say, *That where there is an absolute Acquittal, he should be liable to the Appeal, therefore much more where he is convicted of Manslaughter, and acquitted of the Murder;* For *first*, the Statute 3 H. 7. makes him liable in the one Case, and exempts him in the other.   2 Hawk. 535.

2. In many Cases a Conviction and having Clergy conduces more to the Safety of the Prisoner than an Acquittal; for if the Prisoner were convicted and had his Clergy, he was thereby discharged of all Crimes committed before Clergy had, until 8 *Eliz.* But if he had been acquitted, he was liable to answer for any others committed before his Acquittal, *Dyer* 214*. 1 *And.* 114‡. And though the Clergy be taken away from Murder, with which he is charged in the Appeal, yet that makes no Alteration; for Manslaughter is the same Offence, only differing in Circumstance and Degree; and at the Time of the making the Statute of 3 H. 7. Clergy might be had for the one as well as the other; and the subsequent Statutes of 23 H. 8. and 1 Ed. 6. have not that Effect as to hinder him from having his Clergy for any Offence for which he was not excluded from it. For it would be very strange that the 23 H. 8. c. 1. and 1 Ed. 9. c. 12. should have those Consequences, *first*, by taking away Clergy for Murder, to hinder one from the Enjoyment of it that is only found guilty of Manslaughter, though appealed of Murder; and *secondly*, to put a Man upon another Trial for his Life, when he was before in Danger of it, which is contrary to the Maxim of the Common Law. 4 *Rep.* 45. *Vaux's Case.*

2 H.P.C. 535. Holcroft's Case. 4 Rep. 46. Co. Ent. 55. 3 Inst. Cap. 57. 2 Hawk. 535.

3. To suspend the Allowance of Clergy, is to take away a Man's Defence, whereby he might prevent the being convicted of Murder, which Conviction deprives him of his Clergy; for, notwithstanding these Statutes of 23 H. 8. and 1 Ed. 6. if a Man had been convicted of another Manslaughter or Larceny, and had his Clergy, he might have pleaded that Conviction and Allowance of Clergy in Bar of an Appeal or Indictment of another

* Pl. 48, 49, 50. Stone's Case.
‡ Pl. 158.

Murder

Murder committed before Clergy had, though ousted of Clergy if convicted, *Dyer* 214. and 8 *Eliz.* The recital of the Statute shews that the Law was so, till altered by that Statute, which by no Construction can extend to this Case, because it is the same Offence.

2 Hawk. 537.

The Statute of 3 *H.* 7. is severe in overthrowing a Fundamental Point in Law, in subjecting a Man that is acquitted, to another Tryal, which is putting his Life twice in Danger for the same Crime; therefore the Purview of 3 *H.* 7. ought to be taken strictly, and the Exception favourably.

1. Because that Exception preserves the ancient Right that a Man had, and the Benefit of Clergy hath been always extended upon the Construction of any Act of Parliament made for the Preservation of it: Therefore the Construction 25 *E.* 3. is, *that as soon as ever a Man is recorded to have read, he is immediately the Ordinary's Prisoner, though remanded to the Gaol, and the Temporal Court hath nothing more to do with him.* St. Pl. Cor. 102.

2. It is such a Privilege, of which no general Words in an Act of Parliament have been construed to deprive an Offender: Therefore, if a Fact be made Felony by a Statute wherein are these express Words, *viz. That the Offender shall suffer Pains of Death,* as in the Statute of 1 *Jac.* for *Polygamy, &c.* yet the Offender shall have his Clergy. *Vide* 3 *Inst.* 73. and many other Instances*.

3. Though the Appeal be attached in the Appellant, yet the Conviction of Manslaughter upon an Indictment, pending the Appeal, and Clergy allowed, will be a good Bar thereunto. *Vide* 4 *Rep.* 74. *Wrote* and *Wigg,* which hath these Words, *viz. If before Plea pleaded he hath his Clergy, &c.* which must have this Construction, *viz. If the Appeal be in the same readiness to be tried as the Indictment, then it ought to be preferred to it; but if not, the Indictment may be proceeded upon, and the Conviction of Manslaughter with Clergy will be a good Bar to the Appeal.*

3 Inst. 131.
S. C.

2 Hawk. 535.

* Stone's Case, ubi sup.

4. It

4. It is fit to confider what the Confequence would be to the Defendant in Appeal of Murder, if he had been convicted of Manflaughter, and the Court fhould not call him to Judgment, whereby he could not have the Opportunity of demanding the Benefit of his Clergy, which he is not to have without demanding it, *Hob.* 189. *Searl* and *Williams*, or at leaft if he demanded the Benefit of his Clergy, and no Record made of it : * *Firft*, it would be an apparent Injury done to the Public Juftice of the Kingdom, in not proceeding to Judgment upon a Conviction, unlefs there be fome reafon in point of Law appearing upon that Record of Conviction that may juftify the Court to advife and confider. 2*dly*, It would be a great abfurdity to try a Man in order to hang him, and yet if the Verdict be fuch that he may be faved, he fhall be deprived of the Advantage thereof, which is to fubject the Life of a Man to the arbitrary Difpofition of the Court, though there be a Law by which he might be faved. But this delay of the Court fhall never turn to the Damage of the Prifoner; for if he be a Perfon capable of having his Clergy, he may plead the Conviction of Manflaughter upon the Indictment, and that he was a Clerk, and was ready to have prayed his Clergy in Bar of the Judgment, and that the Court, without giving him an opportunity to demand his Clergy, did remand him to Goal ; for the Delay or Doubt of the Court, notwithftanding there might be Caufe of Doubt concerning it, fhall not prejudice the Party, 4 *Rep.* 45, 46. *Burgh* and *Holcroft*'s Cafe is full in Point : There the Party was called to Judgment, and did pray his Clergy, but the allowance thereof was refpited by the Court upon a *Curia advifari vult* ; yet it was as effectual to him, and allowed to be as good a Plea in Bar to an Appeal of Murder as if it had been allowed to him, becaufe the refpiting of it was the act of the Court. It would be wonderful ftrange, that the delay of the Court in one Cafe fhall not be a damage of the Party, and in the other it fhould. The not calling him to Judgment is as much the delay of the Court in one Cafe, as the refpiting the Clergy in the other ; both are as much without the Letter, and within the fame Equity of the faving in the Statute.

2 Hawk. 536.

Co. Ent. 554 S. C.

* This Opinion grounded on the Authority of *Searl*'s Cafe, does not feem to be at all made out by that Cafe. 2 Hawk. cap. 36. f. 14. p. 536. and the reafoning contained in that Section of Hawk. is fanctified by the Approbation of Lord Mansfield. 5 Bur. 2801.

These Matters seem to make this point very clear; and being so obvious, it is a great wonder that ever any question should be made of it; yet it is most certain that *Toothill*, *Yardly*, & al', were in 18 *Car.* 9. tried in *Kent* before the Lord Chief Justice *Bridgman* for a Murder, and convicted of Manslaughter, and he refused them the Benefit of Clergy; upon which an Appeal was brought in the King's Bench, and the party pleaded *Not Guilty*, and were tried again, *Kelyng* then Chief Justice, *Twisden*, *Wyndham*, and *Morton*, Justices. Whether they were acquainted, with the deferring to proceed to Judgment at the Assizes, and did approve of it, doth not appear.

1 Sid. 316.
2 Kib. 141. 3.
S. C.

Since then there have been divers other Cases, which in the last Reign were resolved by all the Judges of *England*, *That the Court might delay the calling the Convict to Judgment, to hinder him from praying his Clergy; especially if any Appeal were depending before it was allowed, in order to make the Defendant liable to the Appeal.* One was the Case of *Goring* and *Deering*, where the Defendant pleaded his Conviction of Manslaughter upon an Indictment, *That he was a Clerk, and ready and desirous to have his Clergy, if the Court would have called him to his Judgment.* That Plea was over-ruled, and upon his Plea over, *Not Guilty*, he was tried before me, *Pasch.* 1 *W. & M.* at *Nisi Prius* in *Middlesex*, and again convicted of Manslaughter, and the burning of his Hand was pardoned. I did not hear the Reasons of that Judgment, but I suppose that Precedent of *Tothill* and *Yardley*, which was made by so great a Man as my Lord *Bridgman*, who possibly might do it only to have the Point solemnly settled and determined, and some other subsequent instances in pursuance thereof, did prevail: But notwithstanding what had been so practised, and afterwards so solemnly resolved, we did, upon the Reasons before mentioned, resolve, *That the Defendant Lisle's Plea to the Appeal was a good Bar*, and gave Judgment for the Defendant.

2 Hawk. 536.
Trim. 15.
3 Mod. 156.
Carth. 16.
Comb. 89.
2 Show. 507.
S. C.

From

From the Matter of this Debate may be drawn thefe four Conclufions:

1. If one be indicted for Murder, and thereupon convicted of Manflaughter, and the Court will not call him to Judgment, but continue him over to another Gaol Delivery, upon a *Curia advifare vult de Judicio*, &c. if an Appeal of Murder be brought, he may plead his Conviction, and his being a Clerk and ready to real if the Court would have allowed him.

2. When the Indictment and Conviction of Manflaughter and Appeal are removed into the King's Bench, that Court is bound *ex officio*, to call the party to Judgment, and if he pray his Clergy, to allow it to him, and order him to be burned in the Hand.

3. When at the fame Seffions or Affizes there is an Indictment and an Appeal depending, it is moft juft to proceed upon the Appeal, if the Profecutor defires it, and the Court in Juftice is obliged thereunto; becaufe the *Stat.* 3 *H.* 7. doth not forbid it, for the Words are, *That there fhall be no tarrying for the Appeal;* but if the Appeal be ready, it ought to have the preference: Yet if the Court fhould proceed to try the Prifoner upon the Indictment, before he be tried upon the Appeal, and he be convicted of Manflaughter, and hath his Clergy, it will be a good Bar to the Appeal; for there may be a juft Caufe for the Court to prefer the Indictment to the Appeal; as, if the Court fhall find that there is like to be a feint or a covenous Profecution of the Appeal; in order to acquit the Party; for the Intereft of the Crown, and the fake of Publick Juftice, the Court ought to try the Prifoner upon the Indictment rather than upon the Appeal, for otherwife the Acquittal upon a feint Profecution will conclude the King.

2 Hawk. 535. But vide 3 Inft. 131.

4. If upon an Indictment of Murder the Party is convicted of Manflaughter, and immediately after, at the fame Gaol Delivery, the Wife or Heir of the deceafed

ceased shall put in an Appeal, it is most just for the Court to call the Convict to Judgment upon the Indictment, and to allow him his Clergy, before he be put to answer to the Appeal, and then he may plead the Conviction and Clergy in Bar of the Appeal; for though it be the same Sessions, and the Appeal hath relation to the first Day of the Sessions as well as the Indictment, yet there being a Record of a proceeding upon the Indictment it is pleadable in Bar, and may be averred to be the same Day before the Appeal commenced; or if the Appeal be commenced before the Trial, if it appears to the Court the Conviction was before Plea pleaded to the Appeal, it is sufficient: For, suppose a Man is indicted of Murder, and tried, and convicted of Manslaughter, or acquitted, and at the same Sessions or Assizes there is a Coroners Inquest, he may plead his former Acquittal or Conviction in Bar of the other; though the Course now used to prevent that Trouble, is to charge the Jury with both Inquisitions at the same Time, yet anciently it was otherwise; and if the Court will not allow the Convict of Manslaughter his Clergy, he may insist upon it before he answers to the Appeal.

Note, *These Reasons were not solemnly delivered in Court, but afterwards were put in order and form by the Chief Justice.* *

* Sir John Holt who was the original Editor of these Reports.

TERM.

TERM. PASCH.

13 W. 3.

Rex verſus *Flummer*.   12 Mod. 627.
S. C.

Coram Rege inter placita Coronæ Rot. 25.

*P*LUMMER the Priſoner was indicted at the Aſſizes held for the County of *Kent*, 29th of *July*, 18 *Will*. 3. The Indictment ſets forth that *John Glover*, and *Benjamin Plummer* the Priſoner, and others, 13 *March* 12 *Wil.* 3. did of Malice forethought make an Aſſault upon *John Harding*, and that *John Glover* having a certain Fuzee in his Hand charged with Gunpowder and Bullet, did felonioully, voluntarily and of his Malice forethought, diſcharge the ſame againſt the ſaid *John Harding*, and thereby gave him a mortal Wound of which he inſtantly died. And that *Benjamin Plummer* the Priſoner and others of their Malice forethought, did aid, abet and aſſiſt the ſaid *John Glover* in committing the Murder aforeſaid. *Benjamin Plummer* pleaded *Not Guilty*, and the Jury did find this ſpecial Verdict, *viz*,

That *Joſeph Beverton* was duly appointed to ſeize and apprehend all ſuch Wool of the growth of this Kingdom, that ſhould be carried to be tranſported into Parts beyond the Seas, and alſo all ſuch Perſons as ſhould carry the Wool in order to be tranſported. And that *Benjamin Plummer*, *John Harding*, and others whoſe Names are unknown,

unknown to the Number of eight Persons, the said 13 of *March* about 12 of the Clock at Night, about — Miles from the Sea, did load three Horses with eight Hundred Pounds of Wool of the growth of *England*, in order to transport it into France. And *Joseph Beverton* having Notice thereof, came with divers other Persons to his assistance, to a certain Lane about 7 Miles distant from the Sea, in order to stop and seize the Wool so intended to be transported, and placed themselves in divers Places about the Lane; and *Joseph Beverton* with his Company hearing the three Horses laden with Wool, pronounced a Watch Word agreed on between him and his Assistants; and thereupon all of them used their utmost endeavour to seize the Wool, whereupon one of the eight Persons in company with *Benjamin Plummer*, whose Name is unknown, did shoot off the Fuzee, and thereby did kill the said *John Harding*, being one of the eight Persons, and a Partner with them in the Design of transporting the Wool, of which Wound he died.

The Question is upon this special Verdict, Whether *Benjamin Plummer* be guilty of the Murder as charged in the Indictment, or so much as of the Death of *John Harding*.

To put the Case in as few Words as may be, so as to bring it to a Point, it is no more than this. Eight Persons had loaded a quantity of Wool to carry it to be transported; of which the King's Officers having Intelligence, did in the Night time, as they were carrying the Wool, meet to oppose, and to apprehend them, and they met in a Lane, and upon a Watch Word given by the King's Officers, one of the eight Persons shot off a Fuzee, and killed another of the eight Persons, whether the others of the Eight (besides him that shot off the Gun) be guilty of the Murder of the Person slain?

Upon

Upon this Question all the Judges have been consulted, and we are all of Opinion, that *Benjamin Plummer* is not guilty of the Murder of *John Harding*. The Reasons of the Judgment were given by the Chief Justice.

1. It doth not appear by the finding of this Special Verdict, that *Glover* or the Person unknown that shot off the Gun, did discharge it against any of the King's Officers but it might be for ought appears for another Purpose; though upon the particular circumstances in the special Verdict, there is an Evidence that the Gun was discharged against the King's Officers, and so it might reasonably be intended, considering they were all armed, and in Prosecution of an unlawful Act in the Night, which they designed to justify, and maintain by Force; especially when the Gun was shot off upon the Watch Word given, the King's Officers were endeavouring to seize the Wool; the Jury thereupon might well have found that the Fuzee was discharged against the King's Officers; but since they have not found that Matter, we are confined to what they have found positively, and are not to judge the Law upon Evidence of a Fact, but upon the Fact as it is found.

_{2 Hawk. 627.}

Therefore it is fit to consider in this Case, 1. What Crime it is in the Party that shot off the Gun that killed *Harding*.

2. How far the rest of his Company that were with him shall be concerned in the Guilt of it.

1. He was upon an unlawful Design, and if he had in pursuance thereof discharged the Fuzee against any of the King's Officers that came to resist him in the Prosecution of that Design, and by Accident had killed one of his own Accomplices, it would have been Murder in him. As if a Man out of Malice to *A.* shoots at him to kill him, but misses him and kills *B.* it is no less a Murder than if he had killed the Person intended.

_{Fost. 261.}

Dyer

Dyer 128.* *Cromp.* 101.‡ *Plowden's Com.* 457. *Saunder's Cafe*, 9 *Rep.* 91. *Agnes Gores's Cafe.*

But 2. It not appearing that he difcharged his Fuzee againft the King's Officer, it may be that he difcharged it either out of fome Provocation from *Harding*, or wilfully out of fome precedent Malice againft him.

1. It feems to me hard upon a fpecial Verdict to conftrue that the Fuzee went off by Accident, but it muft be underftood to be voluntary; though even in any Indictment for Manflaughter it is requifite that it fhould be averred that he difcharged it voluntarily; but in a Verdict it need not be fo alleged, but the faying he did it muft be underftood to be with, and not againft his Will; for where any one upon any killing of a Man is to be difcharged by an involuntary killing, it muft be fo found, without which it muft be underftood to be voluntary; for a Man being a free Agent, if he be found to do any Act, it muft be fuppofed to be with his Will, unlefs it be fpecially, and particularly found to be againft his Will. Therefore when a Man is indicted for a voluntary killing, if he did kill the Man by mifadventure, the fpecial Circumftances of the Cafe muft be found, that it may appear to the Court to be by accident.

12 Mod. 628.

12 Mod. 629.

2. But in the next Place, fuppofe that he that fhot off the Fuzee did it out of Malice prepenfed againft the Perfon flain, whereby it would be Murder in him. Then the Queftion will be, whether the reft of his Accomplices fhall be adjudged to be principals to him, as Aiders, Abettors or Affifters to that Murder. And we all held that they would not be Principals: For though they are all engaged upon an unlawful Act, and while they were actually in it, this Murder is committed by one of the Company fo engaged, yet it does not appear to be done in Profecution of that unlawful Act, but it may be upon another Account, and thofe who are in the unlawful Act, not knowing of the Defign that killed the other his Companion

Hawk. 128. in not.

* Pl. 60.   ‡ Pl. 474.

panion cannot be Guilty of it. This Notion that hath been received, that if divers Persons be engaged in an unlawful Act, and one of them kills another, it shall be Murder in all the Rest, is very true; but it must be admitted with several Qualifications. First, the Abettor must know of the malicious Design of the Party killing; as for the Purpose *A.* and *B.* having Malice engage in a Duel, *C.* a stranger, of a sudden takes part with *A.* who kills *B.* it is but Manslaughter in *C.* because he knew not of the Malice, though it be Murder in *A.* 14 *Jac.* Sir *Ferdinando Cary's Case, Plo. Com.* 101. *Crom.* 23.

If divers Men lie in wait to beat a particular Person, and one of them, while they are in Prosecution of that unlawful Design, out of Malice he had to another of his Companions, finding an Opportunity, kills him, the Rest are not concerned in the guilt of the Fact.

At the Sessions at the *Old Baily, December* 1664. The Case upon the Evidence was, that the Secretary of State made a Warrant to apprehend divers suspected Persons, which was directed to a Messenger, who having Notice that they were in an House, desired several Soldiers to assist him in the apprehending of them, but in the doing thereof they broke open the Doors, and some of the Soldiers stole some Goods. It was held that the Warrant then produced was not sufficient to break open the Doors of the House without a Civil Officer. Secondly, though the breaking open the Door was an unlawful Act, of which all were guilty; yet was it Felony only in those that stole the Goods, or knew of the Design of stealing, and consented to it; but not in the others that were concerned in breaking open the Doors: No more in this Case can the Rest of the Company be said to be guilty of the killing of *Harding,* unless they knew of the Person's Design to kill him.

2. The killing must be in pursuance of that unlawful Act, and not collateral to it. As for the Purpose, if divers come to hunt in a Park, and the Keeper commands

mands them to stand, and resist them; if one of the Company kills the Keeper, it is not only Murder in him, but in all the Rest then present, that came upon that Design, for it was done in pursuance of the unlawful Act, 2 *Roll* 120. *Palm.* 35. the Case of *Wormal* and *Tristram*, and in the other Books before referred to. Lord *Dacre's Case, Moor* 86.

But suppose that they coming into the Park to hunt, before they see the Keeper, there is an accidental Quarrel happens amongst them, and one kills the other, it will not be Murder but Manslaughter; and in the Rest that were not concerned in that Quarrel it will not be Felony. So if one kills his Companion upon a former Malice, the others will not be concerned in it, therefore cannot be Abettors because strangers to the Design. And that for ought appears might be this Case, for my Brother *Gould* that tried this Cause informs us, that there was some Reason to believe that he that discharged the Fuzee against the Persons slain, did it upon the account that he conceived that the other had betrayed their Design; and no doubt it was Murder in him that shot off the Fuzee, but not in the others unless privy to his Purpose, for it was not done in Prosecution of that unlawful Act; but if he had shot off his Gun against the King's Officers, and by accident had killed one of his own Party, all the Rest of them would have been Abettors and Principals.

Dyer 128. *p.* 60. This Case is put, *A.* and *B.* are fighting together out of Malice prepensed, *C.* comes to part them, and *A.* kills *C.* this is Murder in *A.* and some said in *B.* also, but the major Number were of a contrary Opinion; for though *B.* was engaged in an unlawful Act as well as *A.* yet the killing of *C.* by *A.* was not in pursuance of, but collateral to it, but the killing of *C.* by *A.* was Murder, because he killed one doing his Duty which was endeavouring to keep the Peace; and would have hindered him from killing *B.* against whom he had Malice.

3. There is another Qualification of this Rule, that the doing an unlawful Act whereby a Person is slain shall make the killer to be a Murderer, is, that the unlawful Act ought to be *deliberate*. For if it be sudden, as upon an Affray that suddenly falls out, and the Parties are divided amongst themselves and fall to fighting, and one kills the other it is but Manslaughter. So if upon a sudden Affray the Constable or other Person comes to keep the Peace, and some knowing him to be the Constable or Person coming to keep the Peace shall kill him, it is Murder in him and all that assisted him in the doing of it; but in others that continue the Affray, and knew not that the Constable, or other Person was coming to keep the Peace, it will be no Crime: For first, though the Constable did not keep the Peace, it is necessary that the Parties engaged in the Tumult have Notice that he comes for that Purpose, otherwise the killing him will not be Murder, but only Manslaughter in him that kills him, and in consequence no Crime in the Person that did not know him to be there, and did not contribute towards his death. At the *Sessions* after *Hillary Term*, 19 *Car.* 2. *Thompson* and his Wife were fighting together in the House of *Allen Daws*, who seeing them fighting, came in and endeavoured to part them, thereupon *Thompson* thrust away *Daws*, and threw him down upon an Iron in the Chimney which broke one of his Ribs, of which he died; this upon a special Verdict was held to be only Manslaughter, though the Peace was broke, and the Person slain came only to keep the Peace; and it is the same if he had been Constable. But then it was resolved, that if the Constable or other Person come to keep the Peace be killed, it is necessary that the Person that kills him do know, or be acquainted that he came for that Purpose. Therefore he ought to charge them in the King's Name to keep the Peace, for otherwise the Party fighting may think he cometh in aid of the other with whom he is fighting. And *Mackally*'s Case doth not oppose this, but agrees with it in the Reason there given, which

1 Hawk. 127.
Fost. 316, 311.
Ld. Raymond 1296.

Ante, 66.
Fost. 272.

Fost. 135. 311.

9 Co. 65.
Cro Jak. 279.
Hugh Ent. 144.

which is in these Words, *viz.* When an Officer or Minister of the King arrest another in the Name of the King, or requires the breakers of the Peace to keep the Peace in the King's Name; if any notwithstanding resist and kill the Officer, it is Murder; but if he had not Notice that it was the Officer, it is only Manslaughter in him that killed; but then by the same Reason the others that are in the Affray, which was sudden, did continue in the Affray, but did not resist the Constable, it cannot be Murder or Manslaughter in them, for their Act cannot be extended farther than a breach of the Peace.

Fost. 351.   But suppose the Riot or the Assembly had been deliberate, and they designed doing an unlawful Act, in which they are opposed by the Constable or any other Person, and one kills the Person opposing, it is Murder in all, *Moor* 87. *Dyer* 138. but more distinctly put in *Lamb.* 234. *George* came with divers Persons in a riotous Manner to the House of *B.* upon the Account of seizing some Goods, and using there some angry Speeches, a Kinswoman of them both travelling indifferently between them to appease them, was suddenly stricken in the Head with a Stone thrown over the Wall by one of the Servants of *George*, whereof she afterwards died, and by much the greater Opinion of the Judges and King's Council, it was held to be Murder in all the Accomplices; and though she came as a Stranger and was indifferent to all, yet they came with Malice against *B.* and in pursuance, and in Execution of that Riot the Woman was killed.

4. As the unlawful Act ought to be deliberate to make the killing Murder, so it ought to be such an Act as may tend to the hurt of another either, immediately, or by necessary Consequence. If Persons are in a Riot, and go with offensive Arms, or with Clubs and Staves, and in that Riot one of the Company kills another, it is Murder in him, and in all the Rest that are engaged in the Riot, though but lookers on, *Dal.* 280. *Br. tit. Corone*

Corone 171. *St. Pl. C.* 40. *Hale** 51, 57. But if such unlawful Act doth not tend immediately, or by necessary Consequence to the Danger of another, though Death ensue hereby, it is but Manslaughter.

Shooting at a Deer in another's Park is an unlawful Act: If the Arrow glanceth and kills a Man, this is but Manslaughter, which is contrary to 3 *Inst.* 56. that holds it to be Murder: But Lord *Hale* 31.‡ saith it is but Manslaughter, and the rest of the Company will be Guilty, for they were all Abettors to the unlawful Act.

The Design of doing any Act makes it deliberate; and if the Fact be deliberate, though no hurt to any Person can be foreseen, yet if the Intent be felonious, and the Fact designed, if committed, would be Felony, and in pursuit thereof a Person is killed by Accident, it will be Murder in him and all his Accomplices. As for the Purpose, divers Persons design to commit a Burglary, and some of them are set to watch in a Lane to hinder any from going to the House to interrupt them, if any comes in their Way, and those that are to keep Watch, kill him, those that are sent to rob the House will be guilty of that Murder, though they do not commit the Burglary.

1 Hawk. 112.

1 Hawk. 162.

So if two Men have a Design to steal a Hen, and one shoots at the Hen for that Purpose, and a Man be killed, it is Murder in both, because the Design was felonious. So is Lord *Coke* 56.† surely to be understood, with that Difference, but without this Difference, none of the Books quoted in the Margin, which are 3 *Ed.* 3. *Corone* 354. 2 *H.* 4. 18. 11 *H.* 7. 23. do warrant that Opinion; nor indeed can I say that I find any to warrant my Opinion, but only the Reason is submitted to the Judgment of those Judges that may at any Time hereafter have that Point judicially brought before them.

1 Hawk. 117.
———126.
Fost. 258.

These Things I thought fit to mention, though some of them are not such Premisses from which the Conclusion

* Sum.   ‡ Sum.   † 3 Inst.

clusion to this Matter in Question may be drawn, yet they all tend to illustrate the Matter and Reason that we rely upon, which is, that though the Person that shot off the Fuzee against the Person slain did it maliciously, and so it would be Murder in him, yet the others not knowing of his Design against that Person cannot be adjudged to be Aiders and Abettors of that Murder.

Secondly, If it had appeared upon the Verdict that the Fuzee had been discharged against the King's Officer, and by accident *Harding*, one of the Company, had been killed, it would have been Murder in the Rest, because it was done in pursuance of that Design, which was deliberate, and in the Prosecution whereof Hurt and Mischief might ensue; and their being together is an Evidence that they did intend to maintain their unlawful Design by Force, and that the shooting the Gun was against the Officer: But this Matter being only Evidence of it, it ought to have been considered by the Jury, but we as Judges cannot take Notice of it.

TERM.

TERM. HILL.

5 Annæ Reginæ

Regina verſus *Mawgridge.* — Holt. 484.
9 St. Tr. 61.
S. C.

In the *Queen's Bench.*

AT the Seſſions of the Peace held at *Guildhall, London,* on the firſt of *July,* in the fifth Year of the Queen, *John Mawgridge,* of *London,* Gent. was indicted, for that on the ſeventh of *June,* in the ſame Year, he did feloniously, voluntarily, and of his Malice forethought, make an Aſſault upon *William Cope,* Gent. and with a Sword on the left Part of his Breaſt, near the left Pap, did him ſtrike and pierce, giving him thereby a mortal Wound, of which he the ſaid *William Cope* did inſtantly die. Which Indictment being delivered to the Juſtices of Goal Delivery for *Newgate,* he was arraigned thereupon, and pleaded *Not Guilty.*

The

Regina versus Mawgridge.

The Jury found this Special Verdict.

That William Cope *was Lieutenant of the Queen's Guards in the* Tower, *and the principal Officer then commanding there, and was then upon the Guard Room; and that* John Mawgridge *was then and there, by the invitation of Mr.* Cope, *in Company with the said* William Cope, *and with a certain Woman of Mr.* Cope's *Acquaintance, which Woman* Mawgridge *did then Affront, and angry Words passed between them in the Room, in the presence of Mr.* Cope *and other Persons there present, and* Mawgridge *there did threaten the Woman; Mr.* Cope *did thereupon desire* Mawgridge *to forbear such usage of the Woman, saying that he must protect the Woman; thereupon* Mawgridge *did continue the reproachful Language to the Woman, and demanded Satisfaction of Mr.* Cope, *to the intent to provoke him to fight; thereupon Mr.* Cope *told him it was not a convenient Place to give him Satisfaction, but at another Time and Place he would be ready to give it to him, and in the mean Time desired him to be more civil, or to leave the Company; thereupon* John Mawgridge *rose up, and was going out of the Room; and so going, did suddenly snatch up a Glass Bottle full of Wine, then standing upon the Table, and violently threw it at him the said Mr.* Cope, *and therewith struck him upon the Head, and immediately thereupon, without any Intermission, drew his Sword, and thrust him into the left Part of his Breast, over the Arm of one* Robert Martin, *notwithstanding the endeavour used by the said* Martin *to hinder* Mawgridge *from killing Mr.* Cope, *and gave Mr.* Cope *the Wound in the Indictment mentioned, whereof he instantly died. But the Jury do further say, that immediately, in a little Space of Time, between* Mawgridge's *drawing his Sword and the giving the mortal Wound by him, Mr.* Cope *did arise from his Chair where he sate, and took another Bottle that then stood upon the Table, and threw it at* Mawgridge, *which did hit and break his Head; that Mr.* Cope *had no Sword in his Hand drawn all the While; and that after* Mawgridge *had thrown the Bottle, Mr.* Cope *spake not.*

not. *And whether this be Murder or Manslaughter, the Jury pray the Advice of the Court.*

A day being appointed for the Resolution of the Court, and the Marshal required to bring the Prisoner to the Bar; returned he was escaped; which being recorded, the *Chief Justice* gave the Opinion of the Judges in this manner:

This Record being removed into this Court, the Case hath been argued before all the Judges; and all of us, except my Lord Chief Justice Trevor, *are of opinion that* Mawgridge *is guilty of Murder.*

This hath been a Case of great Expectation.

This Distinction between *Murder* and *Manslaughter* only, is occasioned by the Statute of 23 *H.* 8. and other Statutes that took away the Benefit of Clergy from Murder committed by Malice prepensed, which Statutes have been the Occasion of many nice Speculations.

The Word *MURDER* is known to be a Term or a Description of Homicide committed in the worst Manner, which is no where used but in this Island, and is a Word framed by our *Saxon* Ancestors in the Reign of *Canutus* upon a particular Occasion, which appears by an uncontested Authority, *Lamb.* 141. In the Laws of *Edward* the Confessor: *Murdra quidem inventa fuerunt in diebus Canuti Regis, qui post acquisitam Angliam & pacificatam, rogatu Baronum Angliæ remisit in Daciam exercitum suum.* Thereupon a Law was made, *That if any* Englishman *should kill any of the* Danes *that he had left behind, if he were apprehended, he should undergo the Ordeal Trial to clear himself; and if the Murder were not found within eight Days, and after that a Month was given, then if he could not be found, the Ville should pay forty-six Marks, which if not able to pay, it should be levied upon the Hundred. Bracton* 120. agrees with this Account.

1 Hawk. 114.
1 H.P.C. 425.
in notis.

R   Though

Though this Law ceased upon the Expulsion of the *Danes*, yet *William* the Conqueror revived it for the Security of his *Normans*, as appears by his Laws, after he had confirmed King *Edward* the Confessor's Laws. And *Henry* 1. *anno primo Regni*, afterwards by his Law (as appears in the Addition to *Lambert*) establishes, *That if a Man be found slain, he should be taken to be* a Frenchman *if it was not proved that he was an* Englishman, *and the Country was bound to enquire whether the person slain was an* English-*man or a* French-*man*. These Inquisitions were taken before the Coroner, and returned to the Justices in *Eyre*, and if the Jury found him an *Englishman*, then the Country was to be discharged, which Law was called *Englishire*, and the Justices in *Eyre* were also bound to enquire thereof, until the Statute of 14 E. 3. which, as it is mentioned in *Stamford*, was abolished.

P. C. 18 a.

Hereby a mistake upon the Statute of *Marlebridge* is rectified, which is *cap*. 26. *Murdrum de cetero non adjudicatur coram Justiciariis, ubi per infortunium adjudicatum est, sed locum habeat Murdrum de interfectis per Feloniam tantum, & non aliter*. This was not made upon a Supposition that he that killed the Person slain by Misfortune should be hanged, but only to explain, or rather to take off the Rigor of the Conqueror's Law, that the Country should not be compelled to find out the Manslaughter; or if he were found out, he should not undergo the Penalty of that Law. For as the Law stood, or was interpreted before that Statute, if a Man was found to be slain, it was always intended. 1. That he was a *Frenchman*. 2. That he was killed by an *Englishman*. 3. That killing was Murder. 4. If any one was apprehended to be the Murderer, he was to be tried by Fire and Water, though he killed him by Misfortune; which was extended beyond Reason and Justice in favour of the *Normans*: but if an *Englishman* was killed by Misfortune, he that killed him was not in danger of Death, because it was not Felony. For, saith *Bracton* (who wrote the latter-end of *H*. 3.) *fo*. 136. *He that killed a Man by by Misfortune was to be discharged.* 5. If the Malefactor was not taken, then the Country was to be amerced. But by the Statute of *Marlebridge,* if it was known that the Person slain was a *Frenchman,* and was killed by Misfortune, then the Country should not be amerced if the Man-slayer was not taken, or if he were taken, he should not be put to his Ordeal Trial. This seems to be the true meaning of that Statute.

But, *secondly,* it will appear to a Demonstration, that before that *Statute,* he that killed an *Englishman per infortunium* was never in danger of Death; for this *Statute* of *Marlebridge* was made 52 *H.* 3. The *Statute of Magna Charta* was consummate 9 *H.* 3. and that supposes, *that every one imprisoned for the Death of a Man, and not thereof indicted, might of Right pursue the Writ* de Odio & Atia; *and if it was found that the Person imprisoned killed him se defendendo, or per* infortunium, *and not* per feloniam, *then he was to be bailed.* Which shews that he was not in danger of Death; for if he had, he would not have been let to bail, 2 *Inst.* 42. *Coke* 9. 56. *Les Poulters Case, Register* 133. *b.*

1 Hawk. 5. in Notis.

Vide the Writ *de ponendo in Ballium*

Hereby I have given a true Account of the Sense of the Word Murder, that it was when (first in the Time of *Canutus*) a *Dane* and since (in *William* the Conqueror) when a *Frenchman* was killed; for as it was then supposed in the Time of *Canutus,* the *Englishmen* hated the *Danes* upon the Account of their Nation that had subdued them, and would upon Occasions seek their Destruction, as they did of a considerable Number of them in the Time of *Ethelred,* the *Saxon* King, that preceded *Canutus* next save one; so the Conqueror had the same Reason to suspect the Safety of his Normans.

After-

Afterwards, as appears by the Confeffor's Laws, *Lamb.* 141. the fecret or infidious killing of any other as well as a Foreigner was declared to be Murder. *Bracton* 120, 134, 135. Murder is thus defined, *Eſt occulta hominum extraneorum & notorum occiſio manu hominum nequiter perpetrata.* With which agrees the other old Books of *Britton* and *Fleta*: Only in Cafe of a Foreigner it was penal to the Country; not of a Native.

Next, it may be neceſſary to ſhew what was to be unſtood by *Homicide* or *Manſlaughter*. *Bracton* 120, 121. mentions the worſt Part of it, which is a *voluntary Homicide*, defined in this Manner: *Si quis ex certa ſcientia & in aſſultu præmeditato, ira, vel odio, vel cauſa lucri, nequiter & in felonia, ac contra Pacem Domini Regis aliquem interfecerit:* If one knowingly, and by a premeditated Aſſault, by Anger or Hatred, or for Lucre-fake, ſhould kill another, this was accounted *Manſlaughter*; if it be done *clacnulo*, ſaith *Bracton*, it is *Murder*: That was all the Difference there was between the one and the other.

It appears, that ſince that of *Bracton* the Notion of *Murder* is much altered, and comprehends all *Homicides*, whether privately or publickly committed, if done by Malice prepenfed. With this agrees *Stam. Pl. Cor.* 18. *b.* At this day (faith he) *a Man may define Murder in another Manner than it is defined by* Bracton, Britton *and* Fleta : *If any one of Malice prepenſed doth kill another, be he Engliſhman or Foreigner, if ſecretly or publickly, that is Murder. This was the Definition long before the making of the Statutes of* 4 *&* 23 H. 8. *and the other Statutes that took away Clergy.* To define *Murder*, there muſt be *malitia præcogitata*, as alſo *murdravit:* So that if an Indictment be that the Party *murdravit:* and not *ex malitia præcogitata*, it is but Manſlaughter. *Yel.* 204. 2 *Cro.* 283. 1 *Bul.* 141. *Bradly and Banks.* So if that be *ex malitia præcogitata*, omitting *murdravit*, it is but Manſlaughter. *Dyer* 261. *Pl.* 26, 304. *Pl.* 56. *Vide Stat.* 10 E. 3. *cap.* 2. The Parliament
complained

complained that Murderers, &c. were encouraged to offend, because Pardons of Manslaughters were granted so easily; the Act therefore prohibits the granting thereof. 13 R. 2. recites the same Mischief and great Damage by Treasons, Murders, &c. because Pardons have been easily granted: Therefore the Act doth provide, *That if a Charter for the Death of a Man be alledged before any Justice, in which Charter is not specified that he of whose Death any such is arraigned was murdered or slain by Await, Assault or Malice prepensed, it shall be enquired whether he was murdered or slain by Assault, Await, or Malice prepensed; and if it be so found the Charter of Pardon shall be disallowed.* This is a plain Description of Murder, as it was taken to be according to the Common Understanding of Men.

Ever since the killing of a Man by Assault of Malice prepensed hath been allowed to be Murder, and to comprehend the other two Instances. But because the Way of killing by Poison did not come under the ancient Definition of *Bracton*, &c. which is said to be *manu hominum perpetrata*, or of this Statute of 13 R. 2. Therefore by the Statute of 1 E. 6. cap. 12. It was enacted, That wilful poisoning of any Person should be accounted wilful Murder of Malice prepensed.

Fost. 68.

One Thing more is fit to be observed, That in all Indictments for Murder a Man is not charged positively, that he did Murder the Person slain, but that he *ex malitia præcogitata, in ipsum insultum fecit, ac cum quodam gladio,* he gave him a Wound whereof he died: *Et sic ex Malitia præcogitata ipsum Murdravit,* so the Murder is charged upon him by way of Conclusion, and as a Consequence from the antecedent Matter that is positively alledged. To come close to a State of the present Question, It doth appear that *Mawgridge* threw the Bottle at Mr. *Cope* without any Provocation given to him; for the Difference was between him and the Woman that was there in Company, and his Behaviour was so rude and distasteful as did induce Captain *Cope* to desire him to leave

the

the Room, where he was only a Guest to him, and there by his Permission, this *Cope* might reasonably do, which could be no Cause to provoke *Mawgridge* to make the least Assault upon him; therefore I shall maintain these three Positions.

1. That in this Case there is express Malice by the Nature and Manner of *Mawgridge*'s throwing the Bottle, and drawing his Sword immediately thereupon.

2. That Mr. *Cope*'s throwing a Bottle at *Mawgridge*, whereby he was hit and hurt before he gave Mr. *Cope* the mortal Wound, cannot make any Alteration in the Offence by reducing it to be of so low a Degree as Manslaughter.

3. I shall consider what is such a Provocation as will make the Act of killing to be but Manslaughter only.

Fost. 256, 257.

1. Here is express Malice, that appears by the Nature of the Action. Some have been led into mistake by not well considering what the Passion of Malice is; they have construed it to be a Rancour of Mind lodged in the Person killing, for some considerable Time before the commission of the Fact, which is a mistake arising from the not well distinguishing between Hatred and Malice. Envy, Hatred and Malice, are three distinct Passions of the Mind

1. Envy properly is a repining or being grieved at the Happiness and Prosperity of another, *Invidus alterius rebus macrescit opimis*.

2*dly*, Hatred, which is *odium*, is as *Tully* saith, *Ira inveterata*, a Rancour fixed and settled in the Mind of one towards another, which admits of several Degrees. It may arrive at so high a Degree, and may carry a Man so far

far as to wifh the Hurt of him, though not to perpetrate it himfelf.

3*dly*, Malice is a Defign formed of doing mifchief to another; *cum quis data opera male agit*, he that Defigns and ufeth the Means to do ill is Malicious, 2 *Inft.* 42. *Odium* fignifies Hatred, *Atia* Malice, becaufe it is Eager, Sharp and Cruel. He that doth a cruel Act voluntarily, doth it of Malice prepenfed, 3 *Inft.* 62. By the *Statute* of 5 *Hen.* 4. If any one out of Malice prepenfed, fhall cut out the Tongue or put out the Eyes of another, he fhall incur the Pain of Felony. If one doth fuch a Mifchief on a fuddain, that is Malice prepenfed; for faith my Lord *Coke*, *If it be voluntarily, the Law will imply Malice.* Therefore when a Man fhall without any Provocation ftab another with a Dagger, or knock out his Brains with a Bottle, this is exprefs Malice, for he defignedly and purpofely did him the Mifchief. This is fuch an Act that is malicious in the Nature of the Act itfelf, if found by a Jury, though it be fudden, and the Words *ex malitia præcogitata* are not in the Verdict, 1 *Cro.* 131. *Halloway*'s Cafe, who was *Woodward* of *Aufterly Park:* A Boy came there to cut Wood, whom by chance he efpying, and the Boy being upon a Tree, he immediately calls to him to defcend, which the Boy obeying, *Halloway* tied him to an Horfes Tail with a Cord that the Boy had, then gave him two Blows, the Horfe run away and brake the Boy's Shoulder whereof he died. This was ruled to be Murder by all the Juftices and Barons, except Juftice *Hutton*, who only doubted thereof; and that was a ftronger Cafe than this, for there was fome kind of Provocation in the Boy, who was ftealing the Wood in the Park, of which *Halloway* had the Care; and it cannot be reafonably thought that he defigned more than the Chaftifement of the Boy, and the Horfe running away in that Manner was a furprife to *Halloway*; yet in regard the Boy did not refift him, his tying him to the Horfes Tail was an Act of Cruelty, the Event whereof proving fo fatal, it was adjudged to be Malice prepenfed,

W. Jones 198.
1 Hawk. 126.
1 H.P.C. 454.
Palmer 585.

penfed, though of a fudden, and in the heat of Paffion. This Cafe is reported in *Jones* 198. *Pal.* 585. And there held, that the Court could determine it to be Malice prepenfed upon the fpecial Matter found, *Crompton* 23. Two playing at Tables fall out in their Game, one upon a fudden kills the other with a Dagger: This was held to be Murder by *Bromley* at *Chefter Affizes*, 27 *Eliz.* So in this Cafe, if the Bottle had killed Mr. *Cope* before he had returned the Bottle upon *Mawgridge*, that would have been Murder without all manner of Doubt.

1 Hawk. 108, 109.

Fofl. 178.

1 Hawk. 259. Inft. 23. 1.

1 Hawk. 113. Foft. 273.

In the fecond Place, I come now to confider whether Mr. *Cope*'s returning a Bottle upon *Mawgridge* before he gave him the mortal Wound with the Sword, fhall have any manner of Influence upon the Cafe; I hold not. Firft, becaufe *Mawgridge* by his throwing the Bottle hath manifefted a malicious Defign. Secondly, his Sword was drawn immediately to fupply the Mifchief which the Bottle might fall fhort of. Thirdly, the throwing the Bottle by Captain *Cope* was Juftifiable and Lawful; and though he had wounded *Mawgridge*, he might have juftified it in an Action of Affault and Battery, and therefore cannot be any Provocation to *Mawgridge* to ftab him with his Sword. That the throwing the Bottle is a Demonftration of Malice is not to be controverted; for if upon that violent Act he had killed Mr. *Cope* it had been Murder. Now it hath been held, that if *A.* of his Malice prepenfed affaults *B.* to kill him, and *B.* draws his Sword and attacks *A.* and purfues him, then *A.* for his own fafety gives back, and retreats to a Wall, *B.* ftill purfuing him with his drawn Sword, *A.* in his defence kills *B.* This is Murder in *A.* For *A.* having Malice againft *B.* and in purfuance thereof endeavouring to kill him is anfwerable for all the confequences, of which he was the original Caufe. It is not reafonable for any Man that is dangeroufly affaulted, and when he perceives his Life in danger from his Adverfary, but to have Liberty for the fecurity of his own Life, to

pursue him that maliciously assaulted him; for he that hath manifested that he hath Malice against another is not fit to be trusted with a dangerous Weapon in his Hand, *Dalt.* 292. *Hale* * 42. And so resolved by all the Judges, 18 *Car.* 2. when they met at *Serjeants-Inn* in Preparation for my Lord *Morley's* Trial, *Dalton* 272. If *A.* of Malice prepensed, discharge a Pistol at *B.* and then runs away, *B.* pursues him, and *A.* turns back, and in his own Defence kills *B.* it is Murder. This I hold to be good Law; for *A.* had a malicious Intent against *B.* and his retreat after he had discharged his Pistol at *B.* was not because he repented, but for his own safety. Full. 274, 5.
1 Hawk. 123. Ante, 53.

In a set Duel, there are mutual passes made between the Combatants, yet if there be original Malice between the Parties, it is not the interchange of Blows will make an Alteration, or be any Mitigation of the Offence of killing. Therefore I hold, if *Mawgridge* had thrown the Bottle at Mr. *Cope*, and Mr. *Cope* had returned another upon him and hit him, and thereupon *Mawgridge* had drawn his Sword and killed Mr. *Cope*, it would have been Murder. Some will say, that there is a difference between the Cases, for that the Assault by the Pistol, and the fighting a Duel was express Malice, but this is only Malice implied. Surely there is no difference, for Malice implied is prepensed, as much as if there had been a proof of Malice, or Hatred for some considerable Time before the Act; for the Stroke given, or an attempt made by Malice implied, is as dangerous as a Stroke given upon Malice expressed, therefore may be as lawfully resisted. This very point was also considered by the 12 Judges at *Serjeants-Inn*, and by them resolved to be Murder upon the occasion of my Lord *Morley's Case*. When a Man attacks another with a dangerous Weapon without any Provocation; that is express Malice from the Nature of the Act, which is cruel. The definition of Malice implied is where it is not express in the Nature 1 Hawk. 122.
Ante, 53.

S of

* Sum.

of the Act; as where a Man kills an Officer that had Authority to arrest his Person: The Person who kills him in defence of himself from the Arrest is guilty of Murder, because the Malice is implied, for properly and naturally it was not Malice, for his Design was only to defend himself from the Arrest.

1 Hawk. 121, 2.

3. I come now to the third Matter proposed, which is to consider what is in Law such a Provocation to a Man to commit an Act of Violence upon another, whereby he shall deprive him of his Life, so as to extenuate the Fact, and make it to be a Manslaughter only. First, *Negatively* what is not. Secondly, *Positively* what is. First, No Words of Reproach or Infamy, are sufficient to provoke another to such a degree of Anger as to strike, or assault the provoking Party with a Sword, or to throw a Bottle at him, or to strike him with any other Weapon that may kill him; but if the Person provoking be thereby killed, it is Murder.

In the Assembly of the Judges, 18 *Car.* 2. this was a Point positively resolved. †

Fost. 295. 1 Hawk. 123.

Therefore I am of Opinion, that if two are in Company together, and one shall give the other contumelious Language (as suppose *A.* and *B.*) *A.* that was so provoked, draws his Sword and makes a pass at *B. B.* (then having no Weapon drawn) but misses him. Thereupon *B.* draws his Sword and passes at *A.* And there being an interchange of passes between them, *A.* kills *B.* I hold this to be Murder in *A.* for *A*'s pass at *B.* was malicious, and what *B.* afterwards did was lawful. But if *A.* who had been so provoked draws his Sword, and then before he passes, *B*'s Sword is drawn; or *A.* bids him draw, and *B.* thereupon drawing, there happen to be mutual passes: If *A.* kills *B.* this will be Manslaughter, because it was suddain; and *A*'s Design was not so absolutely to destroy *B.* but to combat with him, whereby he

† Lord Morley's Case, ante, 53.

he run the hazard of his own Life at the same Time. But if Time was appointed to fight (suppose the next Day) and accordingly they do fight; it is Murder in him that kills the other. But if they go into the Field imme- 1 Hawk. 125. diately and fight, then but Manslaughter. Suppose upon Fost. 291. provoking Language given by *B.* to *A. A.* gives *B.* a box on the Ear, or a little blow with a Stick, which happens to be so unlucky that it kills *B.* who might have some Impostume in his Head, or other Ailment which proves the Cause of *B's* Death, this blow though not justifiable by Law, but is a wrong, yet it may be but Manslaughter, because it doth not appear that he designed such a Mischief.

2. Secondly, As no Words are a Provocation, so no 1 Hawk. 124. affronting Gestures are sufficient, though never so re- 1 H.P. C. 454, proachful; which Point was adjudged, 3 *Cro.* 779. *Wats* 6. Noy. 171. S.C. *and Brains,* in an Appeal of Murder.

There having been a Quarrel between *A.* and *B.* and 1 Hawk. 123. *B.* was hurt in the Fray; and about two Days after, *B.* came and made a wry Mouth at *A.* who thereupon struck him upon the Calf of the Leg, of which he instantly died. It was Murder in *A.* For the affronting him in that Manner was not any Provocation to *A.* to use that Violence to *B.*

There hath been another Case which I fear hath been 1 Hawk. 116. the occasion of some Mistake in the decision of Questions 1 Lev. 266, of this Kind, *Jones* 432. D. *Williams' Case,* he being a Skinner, 668. *Welsh-man,* upon St. *David's Day* having a Leek in his Hat, a certain Person pointed to a *Jack of Lent* that hung up hard-by, and said to him look upon your Countryman; at which D. *Williams* was much enraged, and took a Hammer that lay upon a Stall hard-by, and flung at him, which missed him, but hit another and killed him: He was indicted upon the Statute of stabbing. Resolved, he was not with that Statute, but guilty of Manslaughter

Manslaughter at Common Law. I concur with that Judgment, that it is not within the Statute of stabbing, for it is not such a Weapon, or Act that is within that Statute, neither could he be found guilty of Murder, but only of Manslaughter, for the Indictment was for no more. But if the Indictment had been for Murder, I do think that the *Welsh-man* ought to have been convicted thereof, for the Provocation did not amount to that degree, as to excite him designedly to destroy the Person that gave it him.

Fost. 261.

3. Thirdly, If one Man be trespassing upon another, breaking his Hedges or the like, and the Owner, or his Servant, shall upon sight thereof take up an Hedge-stake, and knock him on the Head; that will be Murder, because it was a violent Act, beyond the Provocation, which is sufficiently justified by *Halloway's Case*, who did not seem to intend so much the Destruction of the young Man that stole the Wood, as that he should endeavour to break his Skull or knock out his Brains, yet using that violent and dangerous Action of tying him to the Horse-tail, rendered him guilty of Murder.

If a Man shall see another stealing his Wood, he cannot justify beating him, unless it be to hinder him from stealing any more, (that is) that notwithstanding he be forbid to take any he doth proceed to take more, and will not part with that which he had taken. But if he desists, and the Owner Wood-ward pursues him to beat so as to kill him. It is Murder.

If a Man goes violently to take another Man's Goods, he may beat him off to rescue his Goods, 9 *E.* 4. 281. *b.* 19 *Hen.* 6. 31. But if a Man hath done a Trespass and is not continuing in it; and he that hath received the Injury shall thereupon beat him to a degree of killing. It is Murder; for it is apparent Malice; for in that Case he ought not to strike him, but is a Trespassor for so doing.

4. Fourthly,

4. Fourthly, If a Parent or a Master be provoked to a degree of Passion by some Miscarriage of the Child or Servant, and the Parent or Master shall proceed to correct the Child or Servant with a moderate Weapon, and shall by chance give him an unlucky stroke, so as to kill him; that is but a Misadventure. But if the Parent or Master shall use an improper Instrument in the Correction; then if he kills the Child or the Servant, it is Murder: And so was it resolved by all the Judges of the *King's Bench*, with the Concurrence of the Lord Chief Justice *Bridgman*, in a special Verdict in one *Gray's Case* found at the *Old Bailey* 10 *Oct.* 18 *Car.* 2. and removed into this Court. *Gray* being a *Smith*, B. was his Servant; he commanded B. his Servant to mend certain Stamps belonging to his Trade; afterwards he and his Servant being at Work at the Anvil, *Gray* asked his Servant whether he mended the Stamps, as he had directed him. But B. the Servant having neglected his Duty acknowledged it to his Master, upon which the Master was angry, and told him if he would not serve him, he should serve at *Bridewel*; to which the Servant replied, that he had as good serve in *Bridewel* as serve the said *Gray*; whereupon the said *Gray* took the Iron Bar upon which he and his Servant was working, and struck his Servant with it upon the Skull, and thereby brake his Skull, of which the Servant died. This was held to be Murder; yet here was a Provocation on a sudden, as sudden a resentment, and as speedy putting it in Execution; for though he might correct his Servant both for his neglect and unmannerliness, yet exceeding measure therein, it is malicious. Every one must perceive that this last is a much stronger Case than this at Bar.

Gray's Case, Vide ante. 64. and references there. Forst. 262. 1 H. P. C. 474.

1. First,

1. Firſt, *Gray* was working honeſtly and fairly at his Trade, and juſtly calling to his Servant for an account of his Buſineſs; this Miſcreant was in the actual violation of all the Rules of Hoſpitality.

2. Secondly, *Gray*'s Action was right, as to the ſtriking his Servant by way of Correction; but the Error was in the Degree, being too violent, and with an improper Weapon. This of *Mawgridge* was with a Reſolution to do Miſchief.

3. Thirdly, he had not the leaſt Provocation from Mr. *Cope*, until after he had made the firſt and dangerous Aſſault, and then purſued it with the drawing his Sword to ſecond it, before Mr. *Cope* returned the other Bottle. But *Gray* had a Provocation by the diſappointment his Servant gave him in neglecting his Buſineſs, and returning ſaucy Anſwer.

The like in obſtinate and perverſe Children, they are a great grief to Parents, and when found in ill Actions, are a great Provocation. But if upon ſuch Provocation the Parent ſhall exceed the degree of Moderation, and thereby in chaſtiſing kill the Child, it will be Murder. As if a Cudgel in the Correction that is uſed be of a large ſize, or if a Child be thrown down and ſtamped upon. So ſaid the Lord *Bridgeman* and Juſtice *Twiſden*, and that they ruled it ſo in their ſeveral Circuits.

5. If a Man upon a ſudden Diſappointment by another ſhall reſort violently to that other Man's Houſe to expoſtulate with him, and with his Sword ſhall endeavour to force his Entrance, to compel that other to perform his Promiſe, or otherwiſe to comply with his deſire; and the Owner ſhall ſet himſelf in oppoſition to him, and he ſhall paſs at him, and kill the Owner of the Houſe, it is Murder, 2 *Roll. Rep.* 460. *Clement* againſt *Sir Charles Blunt*, in an Appeal of Murder.

The

The Case was, that *Clement* had promised a Dog to *Sir* [1 Hawk. 124.]
Charles Blunt; and being requested accordingly to
deliver him, refused, and beat the Dog home to his
House: At which *Sir Charles Blunt* fetched his Sword,
and came to *Clement*'s House for the Dog. *Clement*
stood at the Door, and refused his Entry. *Blunt* thereupon kills *Clement*. The Jury were merciful, and found
this Fact in *Sir Charles Blunt*, to be but Manslaughter.
Dodderidge was clearly of Opinion it was Murder. But
the Lord Chief Justice was a little tender in his direction to the Jury. But *Rolls* makes this remark, that it
was not insisted upon by the Appellant's Council, that
Clement was in the defence of his House, and that *Blunt*
attacked *Clement* to force in: It was without all question Murder, though of a sudden heat, for there was no
Assault made by *Clement* upon him, nor upon any of
his Friends, but all the violence and force was on *Sir
Charles Blunt*'s side.

Having in these particulars shewn what is not a provocation sufficient to alleviate the act of Killing, so as
to reduce it to be but a bare *homicide*, I will now, secondly, give some particular Rules, such as are sup-
ported by Authority and general consent, and shew what
are always allowed to be sufficient provocations.

1. First, If one Man upon angry words shall make [1 Hawk. 125.]
an Assault upon another, either by pulling him by the
Nose, or filliping upon the Forehead, and he that is so
assaulted shall draw his Sword, and immediately run the
other through, that is but Manslaughter; for the Peace
is broken by the Person killed, and with an indignity
to him that received the Assault. Besides, he that was
so affronted might reasonably apprehend, that he that
treated him in that manner might have some further design upon him.

There

1 Hawk. 117, in Notes.
1 Hale 470.
Styles 467.
Quære if the Case be not also reported with some slight difference by Hale in 1 H. P. C. 470.

There is a Case in *Stiles* 467. *Buckner's Case*. Buckner was indebted, and *B*. and *C*. came to his Chamber upon the account of his Creditor to demand the Money. *B*. took a Sword that hung up, and was in the Scabbard, and stood at the Door with it in his Hand undrawn, to keep the Debtor in until they could send for a Bailiff to Arrest him; thereupon the Debtor took out a Dagger which he had in his Pocket and stabbed *B*. This was a Special Verdict and adjudged only Manslaughter, for the Debtor was insulted, and imprisoned injuriously without any Process of Law, and though within the words of the Statute of Stabbing, yet not within the reason of it.

2. Secondly, If a Man's Friend be assaulted by another, or engaged in a Quarrel that comes to Blows, and be in the vindication of his Friend, shall on a sudden take up a mischievous Instrument and kill his Friend's Adversary, that is but Manslaughter; so was the Case, 12 *Rep* 87.* If two be fighting together, and a Friend of the one takes up a Bowl on a sudden, and with it break the Skull of his Friend's Adversary, of which he died, that is no more than Manslaughter. So it is, if two be fighting a Duel, though upon Malice prepensed; and one comes and takes part with him, that he thinks may have the disadvantage in the Combat, or it may be that he is most affected to, not knowing of the Malice, that is but Manslaughter, *Pl. Com.* 101. *John Vaughan* and *Salisbury*.

Fost. 154.

3. Thirdly, If a Man perceives another by force to be injuriously treated, pressed, and restrained of his Liberty, though the Person abused doth not complain, or call for Aid or Assistance; and others out of Compassion shall come to his Rescue, and kill any of those that shall so restrain him, that is Manslaughter, 18 *Car*. 2. adjudged in this Court upon a Special Verdict found at the *Old Baily*, in the Case of one *Hugett*, 118 *Car*.

Vide ante. 59.

* Manslaughter.

Car. 2. *A.* and others in the time of the *Dutch* War without any Warrant impreſſed *B.* to ſerve the King at Sea. *B.* quietly ſubmitted and went off with the Preſs-Maſters: *Hugett* and the others purſued them and required a ſight of their Warrant; but they ſhewed a piece of Paper, that was not a ſufficient warrant: Thereupon *Hugett* with the others drew their Swords, and the Preſs-Maſters theirs, and ſo there was a Combat, and thoſe who endeavoured to Reſcue the preſſed Man killed one of the pretended Preſs-Maſters. This was but Manſlaughter, for when the Liberty of one Subject is invaded, it affects all the reſt: It is a provocation to all People, as being of ill example and pernicious Conſequence. All the judges of the King's Bench, *viz. Keiling, Twiſden, Wyndham* and *Moreton* were of opinion, that it was Murder, becauſe he medled in matter in which he was not concerned: But the other eight Judges of the other Courts conceived it only Manſlaughter, to which the Judges of the King's Bench did conform, and gave judgment accordingly.

1. Hawk. 125,
129.—1 H. P.
C. 465—Foſt.
154, 314.

This Opinion is contended againſt by Foſter 315 to 318, who concurs with Keiling and the three other Judges.

4. Fourthly, When a Man is taken in Adultery * with another Man's Wife, if the Huſband ſhall Stab the Adulterer, or knock out his Brains, This is bare Manſlaughter: for Jealouſy is the Rage of a Man, and Adultery is the higheſt invaſion of property, 1 *Vent.* 158. *Raymond* 213. *Manning's Caſe.* †

1 Hawk. 125.

If a Thief comes to Rob another, it is lawful to Kill him. And if a Man comes to Rob a Man's Poſterity and his Family, yet to Kill him is Manſlaughter. So is the law though it may ſeem hard, that the killing in the one Caſe ſhould not be as juſtifiable as the other. 20 *Leviticus,* 10 *Ver. If one committeth Adultery with his Neighbour's Wife, even he the Adulterer and the Adul-*

2 Keb. 829.
2 Brown. 151.

---

* Although this is the higheſt poſſible invaſion of Property, a Man is not juſtifiable in killing another, whom he taketh in Adultery with his Wife; for it favours more of ſudden Revenge, than of Self-preſervation; but this Law hath been executed with great Benignity. 1 Hawk. in *Notes* to p. 110, *N. Ed.*—If the Huſband, however, detect the Raviſher in the Attempt, the Wife calling for Aſſiſtance, it is excuſable, *ſe defendendo.* 1 Hale. 486. 4 Black. Com. 181.

† In ſome books called Maddag's Caſe.

T   *tereſs*

teress shall be put to death. So that a Man cannot receive a higher Provocation. But this Case bears no proportion with those Cases that have been adjudged to be only Manslaughter, and therefore the Court being so advised doth determine that *Mawgridge* is Guilty of Murder. More might be said upon this occasion; yet this may at present suffice to set the Matter now in question in its true Light, to shew how necessary it is to apply the Law to exterminate such noxious Creatures. Upon this Condition the Court did direct that Process should be issued against *Mawgridge*, and so to proced to Outlawry if he cannot be retaken in the mean time.

2 Hale 305 it is said contrary to this determination, and those of Mackally, 9 Co. Rep. 70. and Oneby's Case 9 St. T. 14. 2 Stra. 766. 2 L. Raym. 1485, 1 Barnard. 17—that he had rarely known any special verdict where the Question was Murder or Manslaughter, Judgment to be given for Murder, but commonly for Manslaughter, *se defendendo.*

F I N I S.

A

TABLE

OF THE

PRINCIPAL MATTERS

CONTAINED IN THIS BOOK.

A.

Abjure.

1. A Pardon void, becaufe no mention that the party had abjur'd - 28
2. One abjures, and afterward (taken in *England*) ftands mute, hang'd, not prefs'd   36

Acceffary, Vide *Principal,* and *Arraignment* 2.

1. On an Indictment of Murder, no Difcharge till a Year and Day after the Fact - 25
2. Of the Fact may be again arraigned as Acceffary *after* the Fact - ibid.
3. On an Indictment of *Felony* difcharges *Trefpafs* - 30
4. Yet of *Burglary,* was again indicted for a *Felony* committed at the fame Time - 30
5. On an Indictment of Murder, is a good Plea in Bar to an Appeal - - 94
6. Neither Acquittal nor Conviction could at *Common-Law* be avoided by an Appeal intervening before Judgment   92, 94

Adjournment.

1. Of the adjourning a Court by a Lord High Steward   57
2. On adjourning the Seffions, Continuance may be from one Day certain to another, but not from one Seffion to another   90

Aiding and Affifting.

1. Where thefe words are neceffary to be found, or not   78, 79
2. Aid-

2. Aiding and affifting *cuidam ignoto* - 10

Alien.

1. If living here is a Subject, tho' not a natural-born Subject 33

Amercement.

1. Of a Ville for an Efcape on the Death of a Man - 5
2. Jurors amerced for undervaluing Goods forfeited - 48

Appeals.

1. A Mute has the fame Judgment thereon, as on an Indictment 37
2. No Appeal could at *Common-Law* avoid either a Conviction or an Acquittal - 92
3. Judgment on a Record of a Conviction of Manflaughter, tho' an Appeal commenced 90
4. Appeals and Indictments commenced at Seffions, are determin'd by the Seffions, unlefs Convictions thereupon 91
5. Appeal of Murder barr'd by being Convict of Manflaughter, and Clergy allowed 108
6. So, if acquitted or convicted of an Indictment of Murder 94, 95
7. How to be arraign'd on a removal into *B. R.* and of a Nonfuit thereon - 91
8. Of the Preference between Indictments and Appeals 95, 96, 104, 107
9. An Appeal depending, not pleadable to an Indictment 98
10. Of Frefh Suit on an Appeal 97

Arraignment.

1. One arraigned one day and tried the next (Vide *Oyer* and *Terminer*) - 8
2. May be as Acceffary after, tho' acquitted of the Fact; Not as Acceffary before - 25
3. How an Appeal muft be arraigned, on removal into *B. R.* 91

B.

Bail.

1. Of Bailing Prifoners for Felony by *Juftices of Peace* 3
2. One convicted of Manflaughter bailed though an Appeal depending - 90
3. The Queen's Bench may Bail in fuch Cafe, though Juftices of *Oyer* and *Terminer* can't 90

Baftard-Child.

1. Concealment of the Death, Evidence of Murder 32
2. How the Indictment ought to be - *ibid.*

Bills of Exception.

1. None allowed in Criminal Cafes - 15

Brokers.

1. Pawn-Brokers an Unlawful Trade - 50

Burglary.

1. Breaking a Houfe in the Night, with intent to ravifh 30
2. Servant

THE TABLE.

2. Servant draws the Latch of his Master's Chamber-door, with intent to kill him - 67
3. Landlord breaks the Door of Inmates or Lodgers Cellar or Chamber, and steals 83, 84
4. No Burglary to enter and steal, the Door being open 70
5. Yet it may be, tho' no actual breaking 42, 43, 44, 82
6. So to break open a Closet-door or Cupboard fix'd to the Free-hold - 63, 69
7. Where it may be of a Country or City House, tho' none reside therein 52, 67
8. Not of a Shop severed from the House, except lodg'd in 84
9. Burglary by *fraudulent pretences* 62, 63, 82

C.

Carryer.

1. Robb'd of Goods delivered him for Carryage, may Indict as for his own Goods - 39
2. Yet if he himself steal Part of the Goods, Felony 81, 82
2. *Quære* why not so, when he takes the whole - 83
4. But after he has brought the Goods to the Place appointed the Contract is determined, and then the taking of all, or part, is Felony 83

Challenge.

1. That they have found others in the same Indictment *Guilty* not allowed 9
2. One Juror peremptorily challenged may be drawn against all in the same Indictment ibid.
3. A Prisoner challenging 36 Hanged and not pressed ibid.

4. No Challenges on Trials by Peers - 54

Clergy.

1. The Court Judge of the Reading not the Ordinary 28, 51
2. Ordinary fined for saying, he Read, when he could not 51
3. Allowed to the Prisoner after Plea adjudge against him 29
4. Where allowed and had, 'tis a clear Purgation and Discharge 38, 41, 93
5. Clergy ought not to be delayed, if demanded - 98, 103
6. How introduced, and why allowed to Lay-men 99 to 103
7. What words in a Statute shall not oust Clergy - 104
8. What breaking of a House ousts it - 31, 58, 70
9. What Robbing of Houses ousts it - 67, 70
10. A Convict of Manslaughter may insist to have it, before he answers an Appeal 107, 108

Confession.

1. Confession may be after *Not Guilty* pleaded - 11
2. On Examination before a Privy Counsellor or Justice of Peace, proved by two Witnesses - 18
3. Such Confessions not to be Evidence against others, tho' Parties - 18
4. Confession before a Privy Counsellor within the Statute 1 & 2 P. M. c. 13 - 19

Continuance, and Discontinuance.

1. Appeal commenced at the Gaol-delivery discontinued by removal into B. R. - 90, 91

2. Plea

2. Plea discontinued on removal by *Certiorari* - 93

Contra Pacem.

1. An Indictment may be alledged *contra Pacem* of two Kings 11

Councellor.

1. A Councellor acting only as such may be a Traytor 12, 23

D.

Discontinuance, vide *Continuance*.

E.

Escape.

1. On Escape of Felons, Township amerced - 5
2. A Felon secretly helped to Escape is a Rescue - 45

Evidence, vide *Witnesses*.

1. In Treason may be of Facts in other Counties, than where the Indictment layes them 15, 33
2. May be privately given by the King's Councel to the Grand Jury - 8
3. Confession on Examination not to be Evidence against others, tho' Parties - 18
4. Where Evidence of the Intent is necessary in Felony 77
5. Where Concealment is Evidence of Murder of a Bastard Child - 32

Examination, vide *Confession*.

Execution.

1. How awarded on Attainders by Outlawry - 13
2. Hanging not pressing on challenging thirty-six - 36

3. One Abjures, after (taken in *England*) stands Mute hanged 36
4. See several executed for Treason, fo. 77. And vide Title *Judgment*.

F.

Felony.

1. Felony cannot be (in taking Goods) without Trespass 23
2. Therefore not by a Lodger of the Goods hired, (*sed vide fol.* 81 to 85 *contra*.) 24
3. May be notwithstanding the delivery of the Goods, 35, 81, 82
4. As a Porter or Carrier who takes and sells, &c. 82, 83
5. A Landlord breaking his Lodgers Chamber, and stealing, &c. Felony, not Burglary 84
6. Goods taken from one place, and left in another in the same House - 31
7. Where breaking a House by colour of a Servant is Felony 47
8. Where, though the Indictment is Felony, the Judgment may be Trespass - 29
9. No Felony in a Wife to join with her Husband - 31
10. How a pretended Wife in such a case shall be indicted 37
11. Where, one attainted of Felony, or burnt in the Hand, may be a Witness - *ibid.*
12. Helping a Felon secretly to Escape - 45
13. Pulling down Enclosures Felony - 75
14. So breaking of Prisons whereby Felons Escape, and in some cases Treason - 77

Fresh Suit.

1. What it is, determinable at discretion of the Judges 96

G. Gaol-

THE TABLE.

G.

Gaol-Delivery, vide *Oyer and Terminer*.

Gaols and Gaolers.

1. Prisoners for Treason and Felony to be sent to *Newgate*, not *Newprison* - 2
2. Gaolers to make more perfect Kallenders - 3
3. And to certify Causes of Imprisonment, and take notice of the same - 4

Goldsmith, vide *Judgments* 5.

Goods.

1. Stolen and sold, restored to the Owner that Prosecutes 35, 48
2. Sold to a Broker does not alter the property - 50.
3. Of the Imployer, may be laid the Goods of the Carrier 39
4. Delivered to a Porter or Carrier, and stolen by him, Felony 25, 82, 83
5. Taken by a Lodger that Hires them, neither Felony nor Trespass 24, vide 81 to 85 *contra*.
6. Taken by the owner of a House out of his Lodgers Chamber 84
7. Taken out of a House before the owner Lodges in it 46
8. Taken by colour of Law, yet Felony - 47
9. Goods forfeited undervalued, the Jury amerced 84

H.

Habeas Corpus.

1. Of removing Prisoners thereby - 4

Highways.

1. A Form of a Conviction on view of a Justice for being unrepaired, and an Order thereupon 34

Husband and Wife, vide *Wife*.

I.

Indictments.

1. Copies of Indictments for Felony not to be given without special Motion - 3
2. Aiding and assisting *cuidam ignoto* in Treason - 10
3. *Contra Pacem* of two Kings 11
4. The Indictment in *Latin*, tho' the Writ in *English* 8, 12
5. Found on private Evidence to the Grand-Jury - 8
6. A joint Indictment several in Law - 9
7. Time of the Fact not material in Treason - 16
8. Where it lays the Treason in one County, yet Evidence of Facts may be in other Counties 15, 33
9. Where it makes *levying War* the Treason, 'tis local; *contra* where inserted only as an Overt Act to prove the Treason 16
10. How Overt Acts are to be alledged. *Vide* Tit. *Overt Acts*.
11. Whe the Indictment is to be for *levying War*, and when *for conspiring the King's Death* 21
12. Printing Treasonable Positions a compassing the King's Death 22
13. Where for Felony it must be *felonice cepit & asportavit* 82
14. Where the Indictment is for Felony, the Judgment may be Trespass - 29

One

15. One indicted of Burglary and Stealing is acquitted, cannot be after indicted for Burglary, but may for Felony in stealing the Goods of another at the same time 30, 52. *Vide* Tit. *Goods*.
16. Where it may say *per infortunium*, when a Master kills his Servant, or Parent a Child   28
17. For Murder of a Base Child, it concludes *contra Pacem* generally, and not *contra formam Statut*   32
18. Indictment of Murder, Conviction of Manslaughter 89 to 108
19. Manslaughter is to be alledged done voluntarily   112
20. Yet Murder is not charged positively, but by conclusion   125
21. Best to join several Criminals in the same Indictment   9, 71
22. Where an Indictment and an Appeal are depending, the Appeal shall have preference, if desired   -   107
23. Where Indictments are more regarded than Appeals 95, 96 *Vide* Tit. *Appeals*.
24. How an Indictment must be laid for robbing Houses and Persons   -   69, 70

Informations.

1. An Information to be against the Township on a Felon's Escape   5

Judgments.

1. For printing Treasonable and Factious Books   -   24
2. Judgment for Trespass though the Indictment was Felony   29
3. Where one standing mute, Judgment to be press'd   36
4. In Appeals a Mute has the same Judgment as on Indictments   37

5. Judgment on a Goldsmith for falsifying Plate   -   39
6. Several Judgments on one and the same Verdict   -   77
7. Judgment on a Conviction of Manslaughter returned, though an Appeal of Murder returned with it   -   90
8. And the Judgment is to have relation to the Conviction only   91

Judges.

1. Their Habit on Trials of Peers   54
2. Not to deliver their Opinion but in open Court   *ibid*
3. *Quære* if asked by the Lord High Steward in absence of the Prisoner   -   *ibid*

Jurors.

1. That they have found others in the same Indictment Guilty, no cause of Challenge   9
2. One peremptorily challenged may be drawn against others in the same Indictment   *ibid*
3. They may find the Treason at another time than in the Indictment   -   16
4. More than Twenty-four may be returned in Criminal cases *ibid*.
5. Fined for a Verdict contrary to the Courts direction   50
6. Amerced for undervaluing of Goods forfeited   58
7. Circumstances inquirable on the Stat. 1 *Jac*. c. 8.   -   28

Justices of Peace.

1. To certify Recognizances, Bailments, &c. to the Sessions   1
2. Turned out of Commission if take insufficient Bail, or Bail where none ought to be taken   3

Or

3. On View of Highways unrepaired may convict - 34
4. Justices, &c. may arm themselves and others, to suppress Riots, Rebellions, &c. 76

K.

King.

Vide *Indictment and Treason.*

1. King's Councel are Prosecutors in the King's Case 8
2. His Death dissolved the Long Parliament - 14
3. Though not in Possession, yet is King *de facto & de jure* 15
4. The King more concerned in Interest on Death of a Man than the Appellant - 95

L.

Larceny.

1. Cannot be committed by a Wife jointly with her Husband; contra of Murder - 31
2. What shall be said *Larceny*, and what *Robbery* - 68, 69

London.

1. Difference between a Fact done there (where Death ensues) and done in a Country Town 40

M.

Malice, Envy and Hatred.

1. Their Definition, Distinction and Import - 126, 127
2. Malice implied defined 130
3. What is Malice express'd 126, &c.

Mansion-House.

1. A Chamber in *Somerset-House*; or *White-Hall*, no Mansion-House; *contra* of a Chamber in the Inns of Court - 27
2. *Quære* of the Room of an Inmate, Lodger, &c. 83, 84

Market-overt.

1. Goods stolen and sold there, may be restored to the Owner that prosecutes 35, 48

Misprision of Treason.

1. Concealment, where High-Treason, and where Misprision only - 17
2. What requisite to make Misprision of Treason, *ib. &* 21, 22
3. Uttering of false Money knowingly, not Misprision of Treason, but a great Misprision, and finable - 33

Murder and Manslaughter.

1. Where a Pardon of one shall extend to the other - 24
2. *Stat.* 3 *H.* 7. *c.* 1. extends to Murder, not Manslaughter 25
3. Party dying through his own Negligence or Disorder, no excuse - 26
4. Murder to kill one suddenly without cause 27, 128
5. And the sudden Quarrel lies on the Prisoner to prove 27, 127
6. Quarrel in the morning and fight in the afternoon, Murder, *ibid.* & 56
7. Intent to conceal a Bastard Child, not Murder within the Statute - 32
8. See

8. See the difference between Murder and Manslaughter 40, 60, 121, 124
9. Verdict for Manslaughter tho' the Court directed Murder 50 *Vide* Indictment of Murder, &c. 89
10. Killing another in defence of a Room in a Tavern, justifiable, 51
11. Poisoning is Murder at *Common Law* - 52
12. Words no provocation to lessen the Crime from Murder to Manslaughter 55, 65
13. What will be a Provocation 130
14. Two playing at Tables fall out suddenly, and one with a Dagger kills the other 130
15. If they quarrel, and after a reasonable Time fight, and one kills the other, Murder 56
16. But if they fight, presently, only Manslaughter ib.
17. *Contra* if they appoint a place to fight - ib.
18. Murder notwithstanding flying to the wall - 58
19. Judges differ if Murder or Manslaughter in *Hopkin Hugget's* Case 59
20. *A.* assaults *B.* (without provocation) by drawing his Sword, &c. and *B.* in defence draws his; they fight, and *A.* kills *B.* Murder in *A.* - 61
21. But if two quarrel and fight, and another runs in to aid one of them and kills the other, Manslaughter - ib.
22. So if it be in rescuing a Youth endeavoured to be Spirited away - 62
23. Master correcting his Servant with a Bar of Iron kills him, Murder - 64, 133
24. So where a Husband strikes his Wife with a Pestle ib.
25. Or a Mother her Child by kicking and stamping on it 64, 134
26. One killed endeavouring to part two fighting, where Murder and where Manslaughter 66
27. *A.* arrested, endeavours a Rescue, and another of his party kills the Officer, Murder in *A.* 87
28. And so in one that comes in Aid of *A.* though he knew not of the Arrest - ib.
29. So where several attempting an unlawful Act are resisted, and one of the Resisters is killed, all are Guilty, though not present ib.
30. But if *A.* yields to the Arrest, and others endeavour to rescue him, and kill the Officer, not Murder in *A.* ib.
31. *A. B. C.* &c. attempting an unlawful Act, are resisted by the King's Officers, *A.* kills *B.* Murder in *A.* but not in *C.* &c. except they knew of *A*'s design to kill *B.* - 111, 113
32. But if *A.* had killed the Officer, or in attempting to kill him had killed *B. C.* &c. Murder in all - 114, 118
33. *A.* and *B.* fight of Malice, *A.* kills *C.* coming to part them, Murder in *A. Quære* if so in *B.* 114
34. Yet a Constable or other coming to keep the Peace is killed, not Murder except he declares, or the party knows he came to that intent 115, 116
35. *A.* &c. come riotously to the House of *B. C.* persuading Peace, is killed by a Stone thrown at random over a Wall by one of *A*'s Servants, Murder in all 116
36. So

THE TABLE.

36. So where several design a Felonious Act, and in doing thereof another is killed   117
37. *A.* without provocation throws a Bottle at *B.* and immediately draws his Sword, *B.* returns the Bottle and strikes *A. A.* stabs *B.* Murder   120, 125, 126
38. What may be done or not done *se defendendo*   128 *to* 130
39. One within the words of the Statute of Stabbing, not within the reason of it   136
40. What provocation may extenuate the Crime   130 *to* 138
41. Ancient and later Acceptations in Law of the words *Murder* and *Homicide*   121 *to* 125

Mute, vide *Tryal.*

O.

Oath.

1. The Oath of Allegiance not properly so   -   38
2. The Oath of a Coroner on admitting the Examination of Witnesses taken by him to be read in Court   -   55

Overt Acts.

1. How to be laid in Indictments   8, 9
2. Words Overt Acts to prove Treason   -   13
3. So is assembling together, advising or consulting   15, 17
4. Whether to be laid in the same County or not   -   15
5. Overt Acts to prove a Conspiring to levy War   -   20
6. Consulting to levy War, an Overt Act of Conspiring the King's Death   -   20, 21
7. So conspiring with a Foreign Prince to invade the Realm   28
8. So printing of Treasonable Positions, *&c.*   -   22, 23

Outlawry.

1. How Execution is awarded thereon in Treason   13

Oyer and Terminer.

1. The General Commission of Gaol-delivery, *&c.* more eligible to try Criminals than a Special Commission of *Oyer and Terminer*   -   7
2. Commission of *Oyer and Terminer* may Sit, Inquire and Try all in one Day   -   77

P.

Papists Recusant.

1. One so proclaimed is to appear in person at the Assizes, and to be in Custody   -   35

Pannel.

1. May be severed where several Prisoners are in one Indictment   9
2. More than Twenty-four in Criminal Cases, and before *West.* 2. *cap.* 38. in Civil   16

Parliament.

1. Long Parliament dissolved by the King's Death   14
2. The Authority thereof no excuse for Treason   *ib.*
3. Sir *Edw. Coke*'s Errors touching Parliaments   21

Pardon.

1. Of Manslaughter not to extend to Murder   24
2. A Par-

THE TABLE.

2. A Pardon pleaded confesseth the Fact, and is waved by pleading Not guilty after 25
3. Gloves due to the Judges on allowance of Pardons ib.
4. Pardon void, because no mention therein that the party had abjured - 28
5. Pardon for Transportation is Conditional 45

Peers.

1. The manner of their Trial before a Lord High Steward 54
2. They cannot wave their Trial by Peers - 56
3. Verdict of the greater number, number good if Twelve agree ib.
4. The High Steward not to speak with the Peers in absence of the Prisoner - 57
5. If not agreed of their Verdict, whether they are to be kept together, or may go to their Houses - 16
6. Those Peers before whom the Indictment is found may Try 58

Poysoning.

1. Of Principals and Accessaries therein - 52, 53
2. The Reason of making the Stat. 1 E. 6. cap. 12. 125

Principal and Accessary.

1. Where one acquitted as principal may be indicted as accessary 26
2. Principals may be absent in Murder by Poison 52, 53
3. Principal Absent, yet Guilty, though he that gave the Poison Not-guilty by reason of Madness 53

Printing.

1. Of Treasonable and Seditious Books, &c. - 22, 23

Prisoners, vide *Reprieve*.

1. For Treason not to be in Fetters at their Trial - 10
2. For Felony not to be discharged during the interval of Sessions, but on good Bail 3
3. Of the Transportation of Prisoners - 4, 45
4. Where a Prisoner brought to Judgment, pleads and is overruled, his first Plea is peremptory - 29
5. A Prisoner secretly helped to Escape a Rescue - 45
6. Of breaking Prisons where Traitors or Felons are 77

Property.

1. A Special Property where Goods are hired by a Lodger 24
2. And so it seems where delivered to a Carrier, *sed quere* 39

Q.

Quarrelling, vide *Title Words*.

R.

Reprieves.

1. Not to be where Clergy is ousted, but in open Sessions without the King's Express Warrant 4

Rescue.

1. By secretly helping a Felon to Escape - 45
2. Rescuing a Youth endeavoured to be spirited away 62
3. One arrested endeavours to be rescued, and one of his Party kills the Officer - 87

Restitution.

1. To the Owner Prosecutor of Goods sold in Market overt 45
2. See Folio 47, 48, 49, 96
3. Restitution

THE TABLE.

3. Reſtitution not to be in Robbery unleſs the Jury find the Freſh Suit - 96

Robbery.

1. Where done by colour of lawful Pretence - 43, 44
2. Robbery and Burglary by fraud 62, 82
3. Robbery of a Houſe before the Party Lodges in it 46
4. What a Robbery within the Statutes that ouſt Clergy therein - 67, 68, 69
5. What a Robbing of Houſes 69
6. What a Robbing of Perſons 70

S.

Seſſions, vide *Adjournment*.

1. Of certifying Recognizances, Appearances and Examinations thither - 1, 2

Statutes.

Mag. Chart. cap. 9. and *Marlbridge, cap.* 25. of killing *per infortunium* 123

Weſtm. 2. *cap.* 13. of Bills of Exception - 15

Weſtm. 2. *cap.* 38. of the return of Jurors - 16

10 *Ed.* 3. *cap.* 2. & 13 *R.* 2. *cap.* 1. againſt Pardons of Murder 124, 125

25 *E.* 3. *cap.* 5. Clerks to be charged with all Felonies at once - 41, 42, 102

25 *E.* 3. *cap.* 8. of compaſſing the King's death - 20

5 *H.* 4. *cap.* 5. of cutting out Tongues, and pulling out Eyes 65

3 *H.* 7. *cap.* 1. of Committing or Bailing for Murder 25, 91, 97, 103, 104

3 *H.* 7. *cap.* 3. of Gaolers making Kallenders - 3

11 *H.* 8. *cap.* 11. Reſtitution of ſtolen Goods 36, 48, 96

23 *H.* 8. *cap.* 1. & 5 *E.* 6. *cap.* 9. of ouſting Clergy 67 to 70, 103

1 *E.* 6. *cap.* 12 & 5 & 6 *E.* 6. *cap.* 11 & 1 *Mar. cap.* 1. of Witneſſes in Treaſon 17, 49

1 *E.* 6. *cap.* 12. of Poiſoning 52, 125

1 *E.* 6. *cap.* 12. of breaking Houſes 69

1 *Mary cap.* 12. of pulling down Encloſures - 75

1, 2 *P. M. cap.* 10. of Trials in Treaſon - 18, 49

1, 2 *P. M. cap.* 11. of counterfeiting Moneys - 50

1, 2 *P. M. cap.* 13. of Examination of Priſoners 19

8 *Eliz. cap.* 4. & 18 *Eliz. cap.* 7. of Clergy 41, 42, 70, 102

31 *Eliz. cap.* 12. Reſtitution of ſtolen Horſes 36, 48

39 *Eliz. cap.* 15. Ouſting Clergy for robbing Houſes in the Daytime - 31, 69

1 *Jac. cap.* 8. of Stabbing 28, 104, 136

1 *Jac. cap.* 11. of Polygamy 27, 80, 104

3 *Jac. cap.* 4. of the Oath of Allegiance - 38

13 *Car.* 2. *cap.* 1. of conſpiring to levy War, &c. - 19

16 *Car.* 2.—for ſuppreſſing Conventicles - 38

T.

Tales.

1. Returnable *immediate* at the Gaol delivery - 7

Time.

1. The Year aſcertained, tho' not alledged in what King's Reign 10
2. Time

THE TABLE.

2. Time of the Fact not material in Indictments of Treason 16
3. Time for Appeals a Year and Day after the Murder 25
4. Time for Transportation seven Years - 4
5. But after five Years to have Lands assigned - 45

Township.

1. Amerced for an Escape of a Felon on Death of a Man 5

Transportation.

1. Not to be perpetual, but only for seven Years - 4
2. Such after five Years to have Lands assigned them in the Plantations - 45

Treason.

1. In compassing the K.'s Death 8
2. One acting as a Councellor only, yet a Traitor 12, 23
3. So if one shews his liking or approbation - 12
4. So acting as a Soldier, though by command of his Superior Officer - 13
5. So though acting by Authority of the Parliament - 14
6. May be found several Years before the time alledged in the Indictment - 16
7. Where Concealment is Treason, and where Misprision only 7, 21
8. Several agree to levy War, and some of them only do it, Treason in all - 19
9. Conspiring to levy War made Treason by *Stat.* 13 *Car* 2. 19
10. Printing Treasonable Positions a compassing the K.'s Death 22
11. Uttering of false Money knowingly, neither Treason nor Misprision of Treason 33
12. What Witnesses are requisite to prove it, *Vide* Witnesses.
13. Several Special Verdicts in Cases of Treason 72, &c.
14. The Judgment therein to be given by the Chief Justice 11
15. Pulling down Bawdy-houses, breaking open Prisons in general, Treason 70, 76
16. Where pulling down Enclosures, breaking Prisons, &c. is Treason, and where Felony 75, 76, 77
17. Nothing Treason in the Intention by Statute, which was not Treason in the Execution at *Common Law* - 76
18. Assembling to expulse Strangers, remove Councellors, reform Magistrates, deliver Prisoners, throw down Inclosures, &c. Treason - 76
19. And so with those that join with them, though they know not their intent - 77
20. What shall be said a Counterfeiting the Great Seal 80

Trial.

1. Trial by the General Commission of Gaol-delivery better than by a Special Commission of *Oyer and Terminer* - 7
2. Several Prisoners for Treason try'd together - 8
3. Their Irons to be taken off while trying - 10
4. Immediate Trial on pleading *non eadem persona* - 13
5. One standing mute, his Thumbs tied with Whipcord 27
6. Where such shall be pressed and where proceeded with to Trial 36
7. On Trials by Peers the Prisoner cannot challenge - 54
8. A Peer cannot wave his Trial by Peers - 56

V. *Vari-*

THE TABLE.

V.

Variance.

1. In a Letter of the Sirname, not allowed - 11

Verdict.

1. Verdict by the Peers is good, if only the greater Number (being Twelve) agree 56
2. Whether Peers not agreed of their Verdict are to be kept together or sent home 57
3. Special Verdicts in Cases of High Treason 72, &c.
4. On one Special Verdict against several Prisoners several Judgments 77, 78, 79
5. A Verdict not so strictly tied to Form as an Indictment 112
6. Where a Fact is found done, it is implied it was *voluntarily*, except specially found otherwise 112

W.

Witnesses.

1. What Witnesses necessary to prove overt Acts in Treason 9, 18
2. Commissioners for the Trial may be Witnesses in Treason 12
3. So may Confederates in the same Treason - 17, 33
4. Where a promise of Pardon shall disable a Witness - 18
5. Two to prove Treason which may be the same that gave Evidence of finding the Indictment 18
6. One Witness in Treason enough at Common Law 49
7. One burnt in the Hand for Felony allowed a Witness 37
8. Witnesses dead or unable to travel, their Depositions read 55
9. So if detained by procurement of the Prisoner - ib.

Wives.

1. Having two Wives, one whereof is divorced *causa Adulterij* or *Sevitiæ*, not within the Statute of 1 *Jac. cap.* 11. - 27
2. A Difference where the first Wife is Married in *France*, &c. and the second here *& è contra* 79, 80
3. She cannot commit Larceny or Felony jointly with her Husband, *contra* of Murder 31
4. A pretended Wife, how to be indicted in Felony - 37
5. Of killing an Adulterer, and the provocation of Adultery 137

Words.

1. No provocation to kill a Man, nor will they lessen a Crime from Murder to Manslaughter 55, 65
2. If two Quarrel in Words, and after a reasonable time Fight, and one is killed, Murder 56. *Vide plus* of Quarrelling Title Murder, &c.

THE END OF THE TABLE.

www.ingramcontent.com/pod-product-compliance
Lightning Source LLC
Chambersburg PA
CBHW030254170426
43202CB00009B/740